INFINITE ILLUSTRATION

GINGKO PRESS

INFINITE ILLUSTRATION

ISBN 978-1-58423-521-7

First Published in the United States of America by Gingko Press by arrangement with Sandu Publishing Co., Ltd.

Text edited by Gingko Press.

Gingko Press, Inc.
1321 Fifth Street
Berkeley, CA 94710 USA
Tel: (510) 898 1195
Fax: (510) 898 1196
Email: books@gingkopress.com
www.gingkopress.com

First published in 2014 by Sandu Publishing

Sponsored by Design 360°
– Concept and Design Magazine

Edited and produced by
Sandu Publishing Co., Ltd.

Book design, concepts & art direction by
Sandu Publishing Co., Ltd.
Chief Editor: Wang Shaoqiang

sandu.publishing@gmail.com
www.sandupublishing.com

Cover illustration by Randy Mora

Printed and bound in China

CONTENTS

PREFACE

> **Marisa Llongo**
Creative Director of estudio m llongo

You see it ... it is an image attached to a word. You did not expect to see it, but you did. You did not want to look at it, but you could not avoid it. You look at this image, and "she," lets you look at her ...

Perhaps the word attached to this image doesn't tell you a thing. Maybe you do not understand it, or maybe it doesn't have meaning to you, but that illustration is already telling you its story. She tells you how it is, and how she wants you to see her. She gets all dressed up. She has a visual language of her own, and that makes her different from the others. Wanting you to meet her, she seduces you, and perhaps gets a smile out of your lips. It might be her beauty or her wit, perhaps it is pure poetry, or imagination. She might have a friendly stroke or a cold one, sober or delirious; she will be what her creator wants her to be. To communicate, this illustration will transmit a speech, she will be the manifesto of a brand whose values or aspirations will be represented in this image.

Like a good traveling companion, illustration in corporate identity will travel with an adjacent word. It will be static or dynamic; it will be the essence of the brand. It will communicate the message we want it to transmit, express emotions and pass on values, and will ultimately distinguish the brand. In this way it will guide words, or walk alone. It will adapt to circumstances, have a family, and, depending on the evolution of the brand and message, will make friends.

Illustration makes ideas clearer, more intelligible, and also gives a flash of light. Illustration makes reinventing concepts possible; it is a resource within the communication and contemporary creation that develops its own ways of conceptualizing images, creating a visual language of its own, and resulting in untold interpretations that contribute to a brand. It is spectator communication, and helps communication flow successfully.

> Arutza Rico
Creative Director of p576

Who hasn't doodled on a napkin to explain something? Who hasn't bought or created an image to dress up their home?
Before humans could write, we created drawings that helped us record our lives and feelings. To draw, doodle, or create images is an experience that is deeply enjoyed by humans because it allows us to express our identity. No two people draw alike. From the way the pencil is held, to the intensity applied, the quality of the trace, the contrast, the chromatic choice – everything is unique and personal. This is what branding is about!

I Brand

The I Brand concept began a few years ago, and was unknown by most designers and clients. The concept was primarily associated with graphic design or advertisement, but is now very popular among people that work in, or are involved in, the communication industry. Creating and maintaining a brand (frequently misunderstood as a business identity) is a constant, daily, long term communication process. We know when it starts, it does not end. I started to become aware of the existence and the importance of this methodology when María Fernanda Morales (branding expert) was hired by one of my dearest clients (Loto) to turn, what had been a very good business, into a powerful brand. From that day forward I have not stopped researching, reading, and applying brand related knowledge in my work.

Branding

According to the dictionary, an illustration is: visual or pictorial matter that clarifies text. In other words, the purpose of an illustration is to beautify, explain content, a concept, text, or a brand. The difference between a drawing or a photograph and an illustration is its communicative function. Taking pictures of food that will be used on pastry packaging is not the same as taking pictures of landscapes that will provide an establishment a certain ambience. Illustration within branding must be understood as any graphic motif present in the brand; these motifs may vary from simple lines (Adidas) to complex characters (Hello Kitty), figures or landscapes, and may be used in greater or less quantity depending on the brand's needs. Illustrations are a fun and universal resource (with no language barrier) that quickly create emotions. They are easy to remember, and may become (with luck and effort) icons or symbols (Nike).

In other words, they help us establish an immediate and strong emotional connection with the brand.

In the following text I speak of 3 projects designed by p576 (my own studio)

Emotional Illustration

Grazia is a place that offers salty and sweet delicacies. For this project, we developed the logo, established the chromatic range, and then had the task of designing the packaging line. The first thing we did was make a very sober color proposal that was within the sector categories. After seeing the results, I thought that something was missing, it looked like any other deluxe packaging line. It was then that I imagined some black and white photograph repetitions, and thought that type of composition was adequate for the style proposed in the strategic approach. I thought of some content that could strengthen the brand; because that is what branding means to me: telling a great story, a good tale. So we suggested doing some visual research involving vegetables and greens. We went to one of Bogota's most traditional markets called Paloquemao, and chose, along with the client, foods to be photographed that could be beautiful when creating a graphic texture. When we arrived at the Chef's home to carry out our research, we made several trials until we made the choice to make transversal cuts in all the foods, because we thought that this produced fresh images. The result was wonderful. More than food, these images are drawings.

The illustrations were used in all the Grazia packaging lines, and its main purpose was to produce a sublime emotion in people. We care little for the charts that explain the package contents. The relationship they have with the product is their profound taste for beauty.

Associative Illustration

Choux Choux is a brand that recalls childhood. It offers ice creams, popsicles, shakes, and of course Choux! The illustrations we developed were inspired on the games and toys we played with 25 years ago, when we were children. Each illustration is designed to be associated with a flavor. I had a chance to speak with a parent and he said he thought the idea of the drawings was great because his son had remembered it and asked for the "little car" ice cream. Another person that had bought an ice cream cup (he was taking it to his sick girlfriend) chose it not because of its flavor, but because of the drawing, which best expressed the message of love he wished to convey. The illustrations in this brand help reminisce and evoke memories and desires; they are triggers for associations within our mind. And what is the purpose of this? The answer is very simple: it was the emotional path we decided to take our clients on, to connect with our audience, in other words, branding. Unlike the illustrations for Grazia, which looked to connect with people with a shared taste for esthetics, the main objective of the illustrations for Choux Choux is connect with the audience through a life stage, childhood.

Relational Illustration

Uva is a juice bar where you can find healthy, nutritious, powerful, but above all, delicious food choices. I carried out this job along with the talented designer and animator Santiago Tobon was focused on transmitting the idea that nutritional beverages can be fun and delicious. Therefore we developed a logo and an icon that had a cartoonish style, based on the concept of a drop and a liquid state. Then we developed a series of characters, which, according to their color, explained the benefits of each fruit and vegetable, and finally we developed the main character "Mr. Mountain" (the execution of this work is in progress). Santiago was in charge of all the drawings and giving each of them their own personality.

These illustrations have a keen resemblance with the object or concepts they stand for, because their main objective is to explain the brand's contents. The connection is made through the need and will of the audience to understand or go further into the concept.

To sum up, 1. illustrations are graphic motifs that document a text or concept; 2. all brands have graphic motifs; 3. they may range from simple drawings of drops to complex photographs; 4. they have a specific objective within the brand's purpose; 5. they are quick and effective emotional connectors between the brand and the audience.

To finish, how do you choose the most appropriate illustration for a brand? As you know, communication is not an exact science and depends on context. Nonetheless, these questions may help you have a clear framework for your branding projects. 1. What specific interests does the audience have in my brand? 2. What is the purpose of the illustrations within the story of my brand? (Emotional, associative, relational, etc.) 3. What is the most appropriate style for them according to the brand's personality? (Line, contour, photograph, engraving, color, expression, etc.) 4. Will they be the main characters, or used once in a while? 5. Do the related brands have something similar? 6. How would they help the brand stand out from its competitors?

I say goodbye giving thanks to Sandu Publishers for their invitation to write this preface, and wishing this text is of great help to people, who like myself, enjoy and want to know more about branding.

Casa del Agua

Inspired by traditional processes, Casa del Agua emerges as a nostalgic brand that evokes and appeals to that which is well made – to the practical, to the timeless, but especially to the beautiful. Man, machine, and nature come together in a common language, unafraid to speak with clarity and purpose. Casa del Agua is the encounter between past and present, and speaks with a high sense of "honesty and transparency." Casa del Agua is also known as "El Agua Local" (The Local Water), or "De Barrio" (Neighborhood) because it collects, distills, and harmonizes on site, CASA DEL AGUA® is instinctively contemporary, yet passionately classic. With conviction, it represents everything that is worthy for what it "is" and not for what it "intends to be."

Client: Casa del Agua | Design Agency: THiNC | Design: Rocío Serna

CASA DEL AGUA
ARMONIZADA
EL AGUA LOCAL
600 ML | PURIFICADA
ARTESANAL
CASA DEL AGUA
ARMONIZADA
El agua es el centro del ecosistema, restaurarla es restaurarnos. Es conductor universal de energía, sus moléculas son sensibles a estímulos y el más determinante es la intención. Casa del Agua es captada, filtrada y purificada en sitio, por eso le llamamos el agua local. Armonizada con los principios de amor, gratitud y respero, alcanza su potencial máximo. Simple y clara, embotellada artesanalmente, es tranquilidad, salud y bienestar. Es fresca, natural y transparente. Es fuente de vida.
ERES 70% AGUA, LO QUE TOMAS IMPORTA
IMPRIME TU INTENCIÓN:
EL AGUA LOCAL
600 ML

CASA DEL AGUA

CASA DEL AGUA
EL AGUA LOCAL
WWW.CASADELAGUA.COM.MX

HaritaMetod

HaritaMetod is a type of notebook commonly used in schools in Turkey. In Turkish, "Harita" means "map," and "Metod" is "method." The name signifies the studio's approach to design: methodically, and following a road map. The engravings are map-making tools from a 19th century book, and the minimalist monogram fuses the initials of the studio to create a memorable and fresh form.

Client: HaritaMetod | Design Agency: HaritaMetod | Design: Ervin Esen

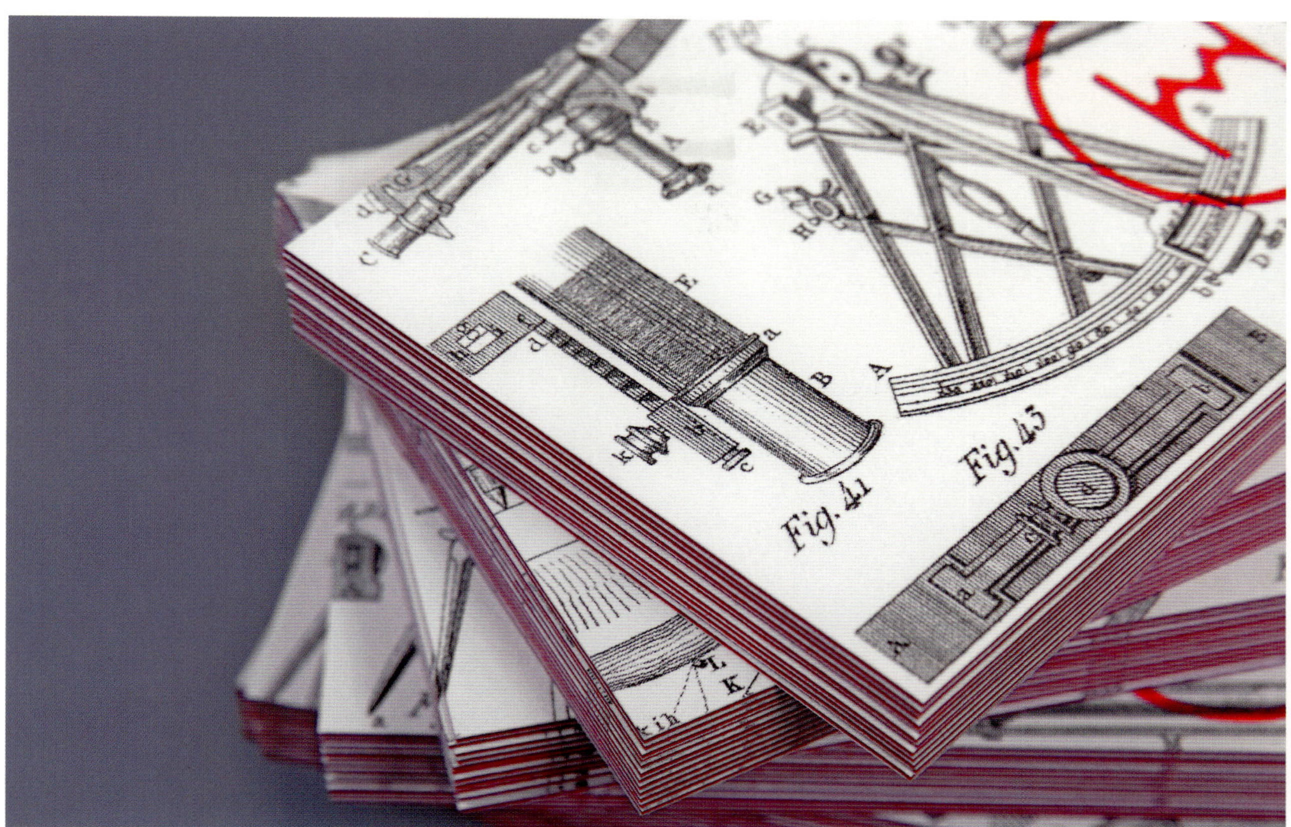

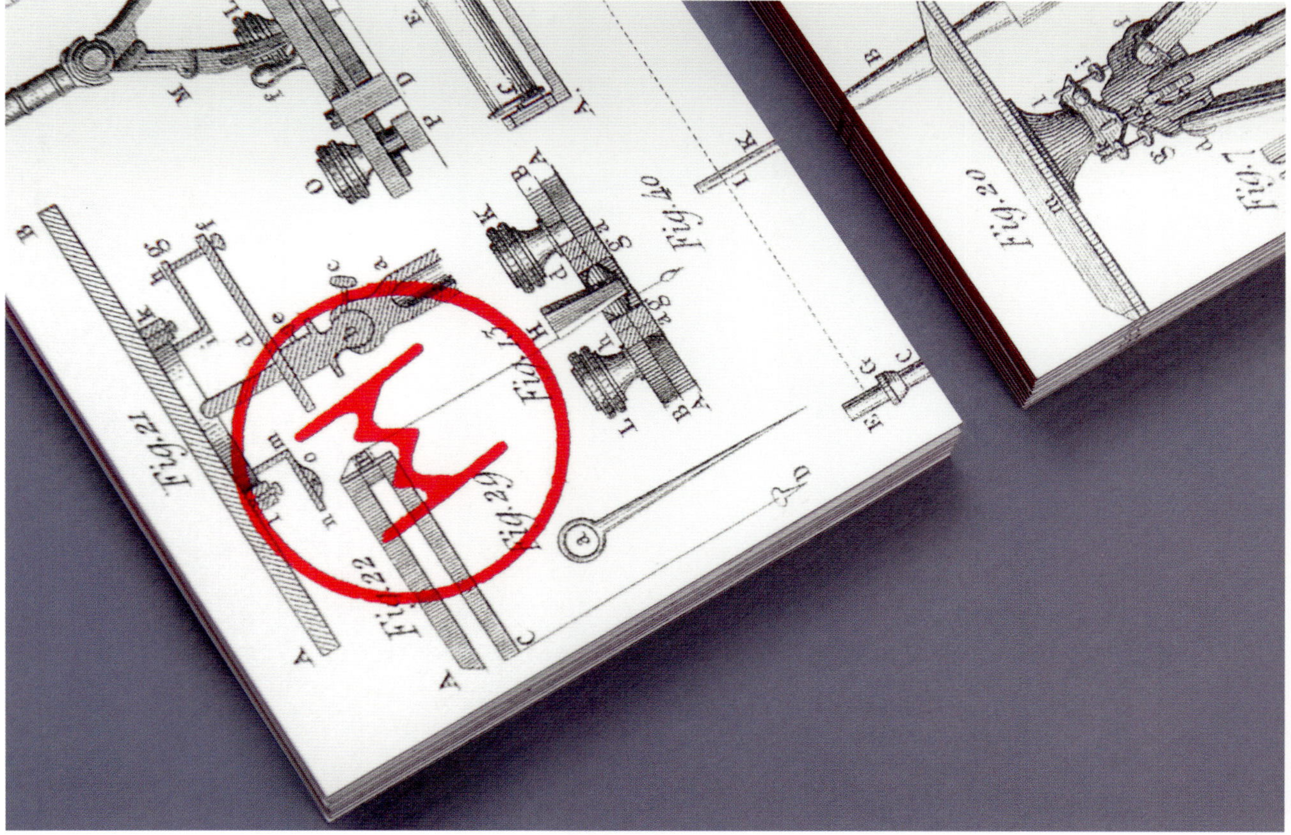

Diana Orving A/W 2011 - You

Marble statues from the collection at the Louvre are reduced to draping only, and paired with a marble texture pattern. Final artworks for the textile prints are also applied directly to the look book's paper, adding brute quality to the grandiose environments.

Client: Diana Orving | Art Direction: Diana Orving, Johan Hjerpe | Design: Johan Hjerpe | Photography: Marcus Palmqvist

Diana Orving S/S 2010 - Curtains

Flower still life images appear behind curtains and on draping.

Client: Diana Orving | Art Direction: Diana Orving, Johan Hjerpe | Design: Johan Hjerpe | Photography: Marcus Palmqvist

Diana Orving A/W 2010 - Light

Bright autumn bulbs shine with inverted watercolor glorias. The fabric print design is also used as graphics for printed matter, such as invitations.

Client: Diana Orving | Art Direction: Diana Orving, Johan Hjerpe | Design: Johan Hjerpe | Photography: Martin Lidell

DIANA ORVING
LIGHT
autumn/winter 2010
Print design & creative advisor
to Diana Orving: Johan Hjerpe
Styling: Naomi Itkes & Marcus Söder/ Link Details
Casting: Marcus Pettersson/ Casting Sweden
Hair: Ali Pirzadeh for RedKen/ Link Details
Make up: Linda Öhrström for MAC/ Link Details
Music: Kornél Kovács
Assistants: Lap-See Lam & Clara Aldén
Models: MIKAs, ELITE & Stockholmsgruppen
Press & Sales:
JUS
+46 8 611 98 00
info@jus.se

DIANA ORVING
LIGHT
autumn/winter 2010
Tisdag 2 februari
Berns, Stora salongen
Insläpp 14.00, visning 14.30
OSA: dianaorving@jus.se
senast 29 januari

Dance Me to the End of Love

Daydream Nation Fashion Print for the A/W 2012 Dreams for Sale collection.

Design: Dreams for Sale | Illustration: Tore Cheung

Last Breath of Youthful Melancholy

Daydream Nation Fashion Print for the S/S 2011 Last Breath of Youthful Melancholy collection.

Design: Daydream Nation | Illustration: Tore Cheung

Neverending Story

Daydream Nation Fashion Print for the A/W 2013 Neverending Story collection.

Design: Daydream Nation | Illustration: Tore Cheung

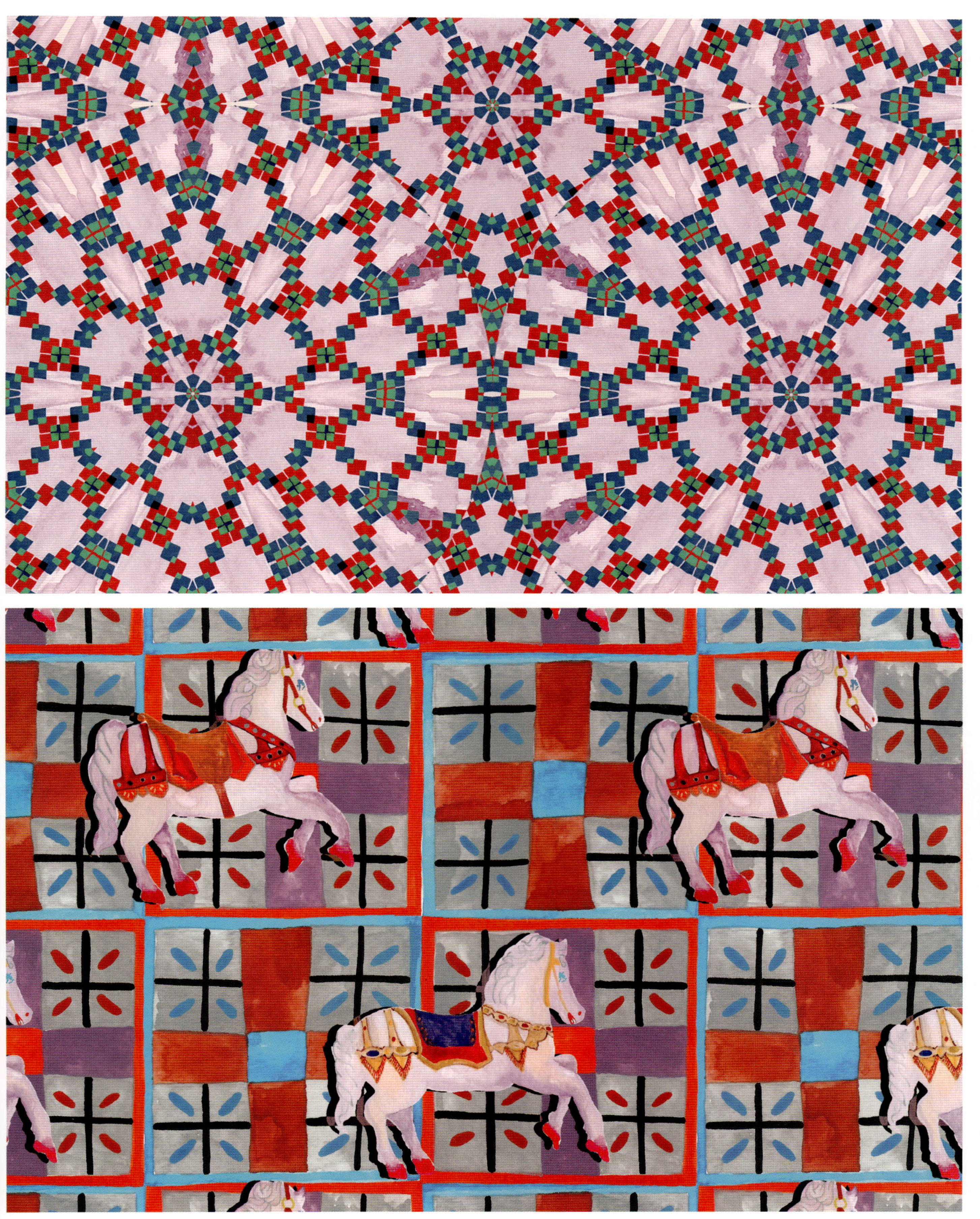

The Show Must Go On

Daydream Nation Fashion Print for the S/S 2012 The Show Must Go On collection.

Design: Daydream Nation | Illustration: Tore Cheung

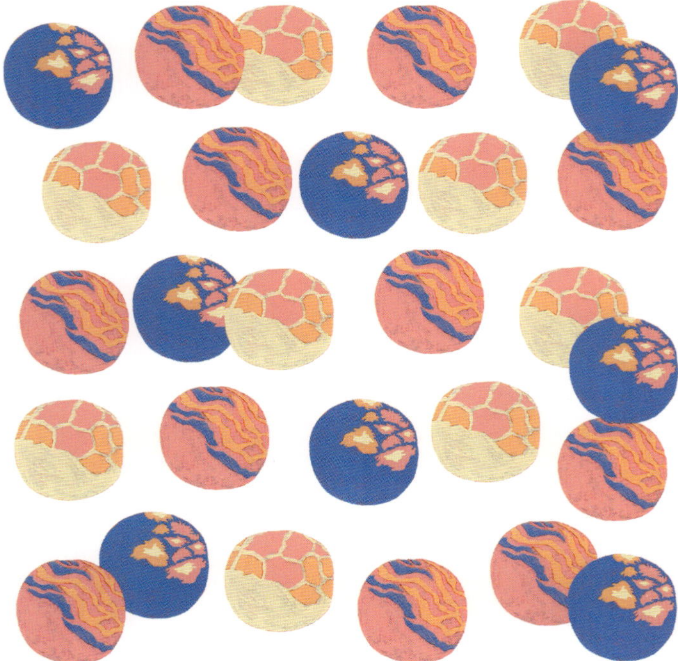

QT Port Douglas

QT Port Douglas is the second hotel from the QT Hotels and Resorts group to open its doors. The QT Port Douglas/Estilio brand and language eschews the convention of an identity by capturing the spirit of place in a visually compelling way – one that portrays a tropical paradise through distinct personalities and avoids clichés derived by "tourist" destinations. Collaboration with Jean-Philippe Delhomme presented a new perspective and sets Estilio as an iconic destination beyond the resort itself. Reflecting the craft and nuances in the illustration, the identity, and it's applications are considered in every way, and delicately crafted with finesse. Overall, the hallmarks of distinction and quality commensurate with an offer and destination that is unique.

Client: Amalgamated Holdings Limited | Design Agency: Fabio Ongarato Design | Creative Direction: Fabio Ongarato | Design: Meg Philips | Illustration: Jean-Philippe Delhomme

QT RESORT
ROOM No.

QT RESORT
87–109 Port Douglas Road
Port Douglas QLD 4877 Australia
Phone. +61 7 4099 8900
www.qtportdouglas.com.au
ROOM No.
PORT DOUGLAS

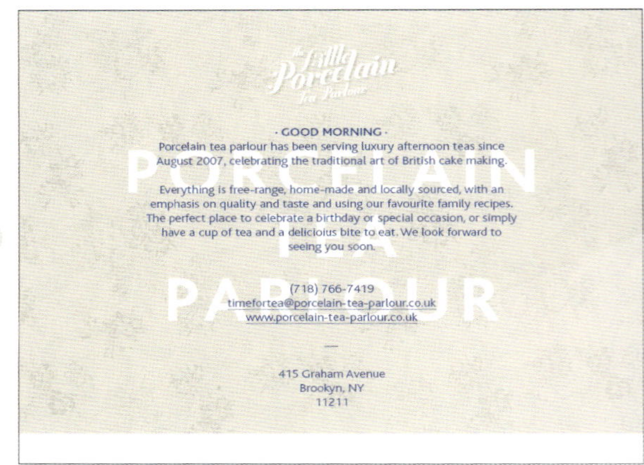

Porcelain Tea Parlour

This project was a new brand and design direction for the small chain of boutique tea rooms based in the north of England. The main visual direction plays on the traditional ceramic porcelain style, which was created by the Chinese and adopted by the English for their china cups and plates etc. These detailed and illustrative patterns were used as graphical devices to help create a brand distinction in their marketing material.

Client: Porcelain Tea Parlour | Design Agency: WeLoveNoise | Creative Direction: Luke Finch

The Little Porcelain Tea Parlour
415 Graham Avenue
Brookyn, NY
11211
—
(718) 766-7419
timefortea@porcelain-tea-parlour.co.uk
www.porcelain-tea-parlour.co.uk
PORCELAIN TEA PARLOUR
PORCELAIN TEA PARLOUR

KLCC
CONCOURSE LEVEL
Bershka
Not Quite An Ordinary Tote Bag
EXHIBITION & SHOWCASE
16/03-20/03
1000 — 2100
ANTONIO SORTINO
LONDON, UNITED KINGDOM
MICHAEL MYERS
WATERLOO, IA, USA
GIORDANO POLONI
MILAN, ITALY
DAVID RYSKI
PULAWY, POLAND
FERNANDO VICENTE
MADRID, SPAIN
TOMSKI & POLANSKI
PRAGUE, CRECH REPUBLIC
IGNASI MONREAL
MANDRID, SPAIN
IRMA GRUENHOLZ
MADRID, SPAIN
OUR COLLABORATING ARTISTS CANNOT WAIT TO SEE YOU!
BRING ALONG YOUR NOT QUITE AN ORDINARY TOTE BAG OF WHICH BEAUTY HAS BEEN MANIFESTED AND SHARE YOUR BEAUTIUFL EXPERIENCES WITH YOUR FAVOURITE ARTISTS! THIS WON'T HAPPEN WITHOUT YOU. BERSHKA LOVES YOU.
TAN YAU HOONG
KUALA LUMPUR, MALAYSIA
EL DIABLO
MEXICO
JEROME ECKWALL
NEW YORK, USA
STEVE SIMPSON
DUBLIN, IRELAND
QUILSKAT
RUSSIA
STEVE SCOTT
LONDON , UNITED KINGDOM
LOG ON TO WWW.BERSHKA.COM/NOTQUITEORDINARY OR VISIT STORES AT ONE UTAMA, MID VALLEY AND KLCC TO FIND OUT MORE ABOUT THE COLLABORATION.

Bershka
Bershka
×
Beauty happens when you do it yourself.

Bershka
Not Quite An Ordinary Tote Bag

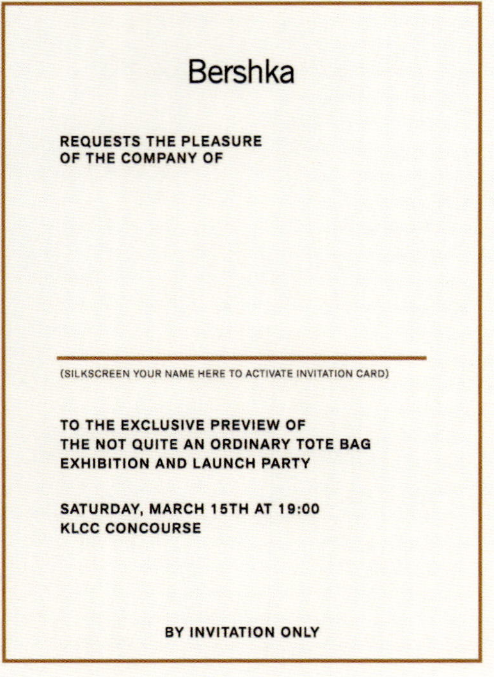
Bershka
REQUESTS THE PLEASURE OF THE COMPANY OF
(SILKSCREEN YOUR NAME HERE TO ACTIVATE INVITATION CARD)
TO THE EXCLUSIVE PREVIEW OF THE NOT QUITE AN ORDINARY TOTE BAG EXHIBITION AND LAUNCH PARTY
SATURDAY, MARCH 15TH AT 19:00
KLCC CONCOURSE
BY INVITATION ONLY

Not Quite An Ordinary Tote Bag

Not Quite An Ordinary Tote Bag is a fictional collaboration project between Bershka, rtists, illustrators and graphic designers. It aims to make people believe in personal creativity and the capability of their hands in manifesting genuinely amazing beauty. In the tote bag, a set of silkscreen printing tools is carefully selected and included to allow people to reconnect with their innate creativity, and to fully unleash themselves in their most unique way possible.

Client: Bershka (Fictional) | Design: Liow Heng Chun

Grazia

Grazia is an eatery in Bogotá, Colombia where lovers of food can buy refined sweets and savory delicacies. The challenge of this project was to create a visual language that honors the beauty and perfection of the food. Design firm p576 began with a graphic investigation of the ingredient forms, which were later developed into a series of patterns for use on all the packaging pieces. "We visited the local market with the chefs, picked some vegetables and fruits, and then went to their house to cut and to photograph the food," said Art Director Arutza Rico Onzaga. She added, "we proposed a second brand element: lines that show the spatial structure of the objects and registers the logo position." These elements, along with the simplified typography, define the brand's sophisticated and modern style.

Client: Grazia | Design Agency: P576 | Creative Direction: Arutza Rico Onzaga | Design: Arutza Rico Onzaga, María Silva | Photography: Doping

GRAZIA
GRAZIA

Merindades

This visual identity was conceived with Navarre Designation of Origin for a retail shop specializing in handcrafted product. The brand concept is based on core values such as quality, authenticity, and honesty. The messages and illustrations traced with pencil on paper relate to the handcrafted goods manufactured in small production by a few staff members. They also invite us to adopt a healthy diet by eating wholesome slow food.

Client: Merindades | Design Agency: Comuniza

MERINDADES
GUSTO NAVARRO

La flor con el corazón más tierno

Muy pronto estaremos a tu servicio
Teléfono 937 961 477 / www.merindadesdenavarra.es

MERINDADES
GUSTO NAVARRO

Rico, rico, gusto navarrico

Muy pronto estaremos a tu servicio
Teléfono 937 961 477 / www.merindadesdenavarra.es

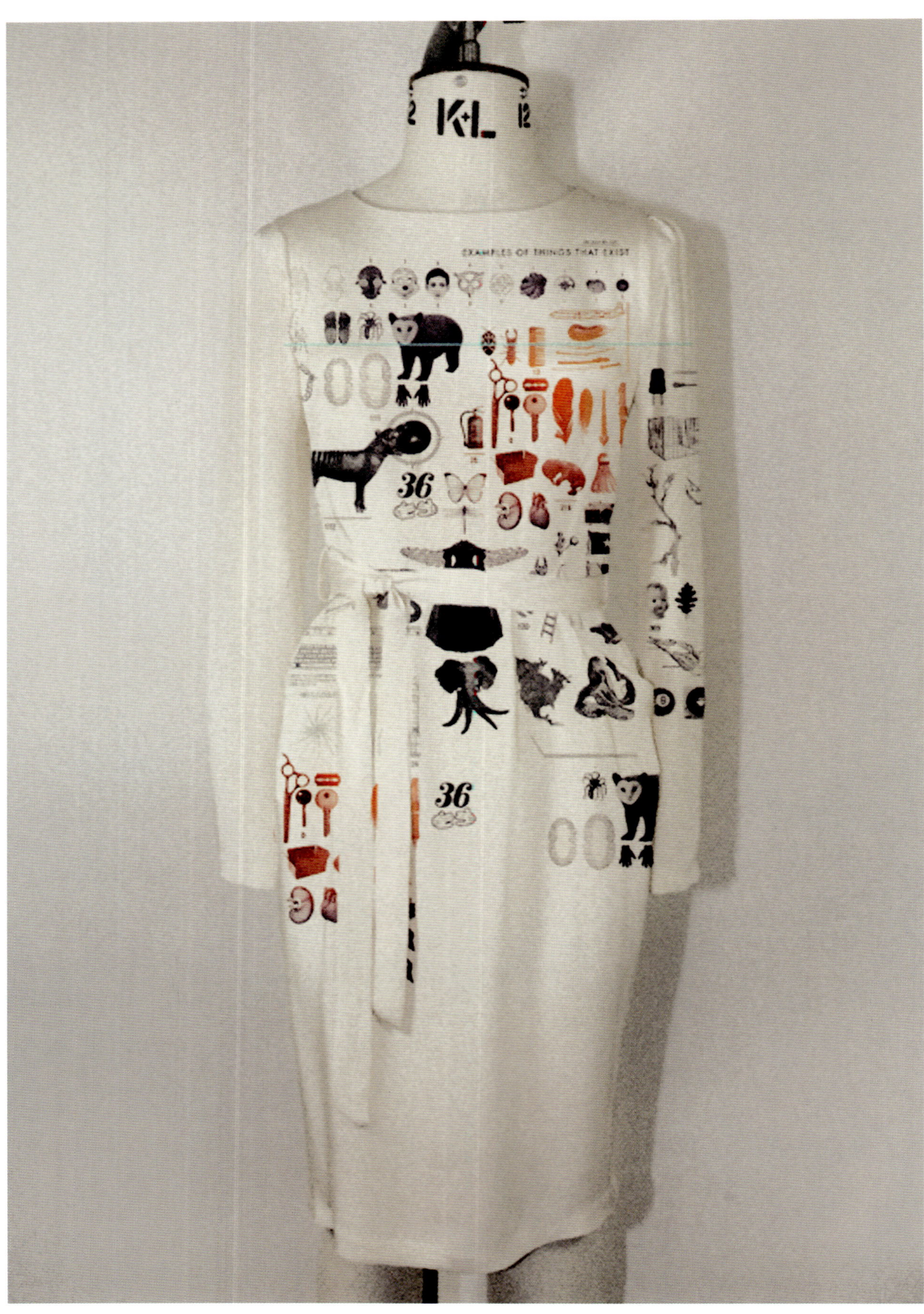
K+L
EXAMPLES OF THINGS THAT EXIST
36
36

Examples of Things that Do or Do Not Exist

Things that do and do not exist is Werksemd's interpretation of the given theme for the project. When starting out with this project, the subject matter of "natural wonder" brought to mind the fascinating strenuousness of collecting and classifying all of earth's species, following the tradition of biologists like Ernst Haeckel or Carl von Linné. The impossibility of taking this whole concept up a notch, to include both natural species and man-made products in an overview of everything that exists, seemed like a potent angle to interpret Natural Wonder in a way that would be sure to fail spectacularly. As the name of the design suggests, even the concept of things that do not exist was thrown in for good measure to further emphasize the futility of the task. The artwork itself consists of a combination of matter-of-fact-ish photographed items and matter-of-fact-ish illustration mixed with a few twisted items, arranged on a wallchart-like layout according to similarities in shape. Round items together, square items together, and so forth, displays an attempt at a system for classifying the objects based on visual appearance, eluding inter-relevance.

Client: Natural Wonder for Border & Frontiers | Design Agency: Werksemd | Design: Nina Elisabeth Børke

Vindrosa Østenfor Sol

Newly born Vindrosa on newly established record label Vagabond Music commissined Werksemd to visualize Vindrosa's crossover musical project , which mixes traditional Norwegian folk songs with foreign instrumentation. The visual interpretation of this musical experiment emerged through a parallel approach where the combinations of well-known objects and materials offers a means of abstraction and furthermore, transformation. The fairytale-derived title Østenfor Sol (east of the sun) is a term often used to describe a far away utopian destination, whereas Vindrosa (Wind rose) is an old Norwegian term for compass. These verbal cues inspired a visual elaboration on fairytale mystery and the concept of travelling.

Cutlery, roots, textile samples, feathers, a pig's ear, a bird's nest, and twigs were sampled and put together in a way that is suggestive of something mythical and exotic.

Client: Vindrosa Østenfor Sol | Design Agency: Werksemd

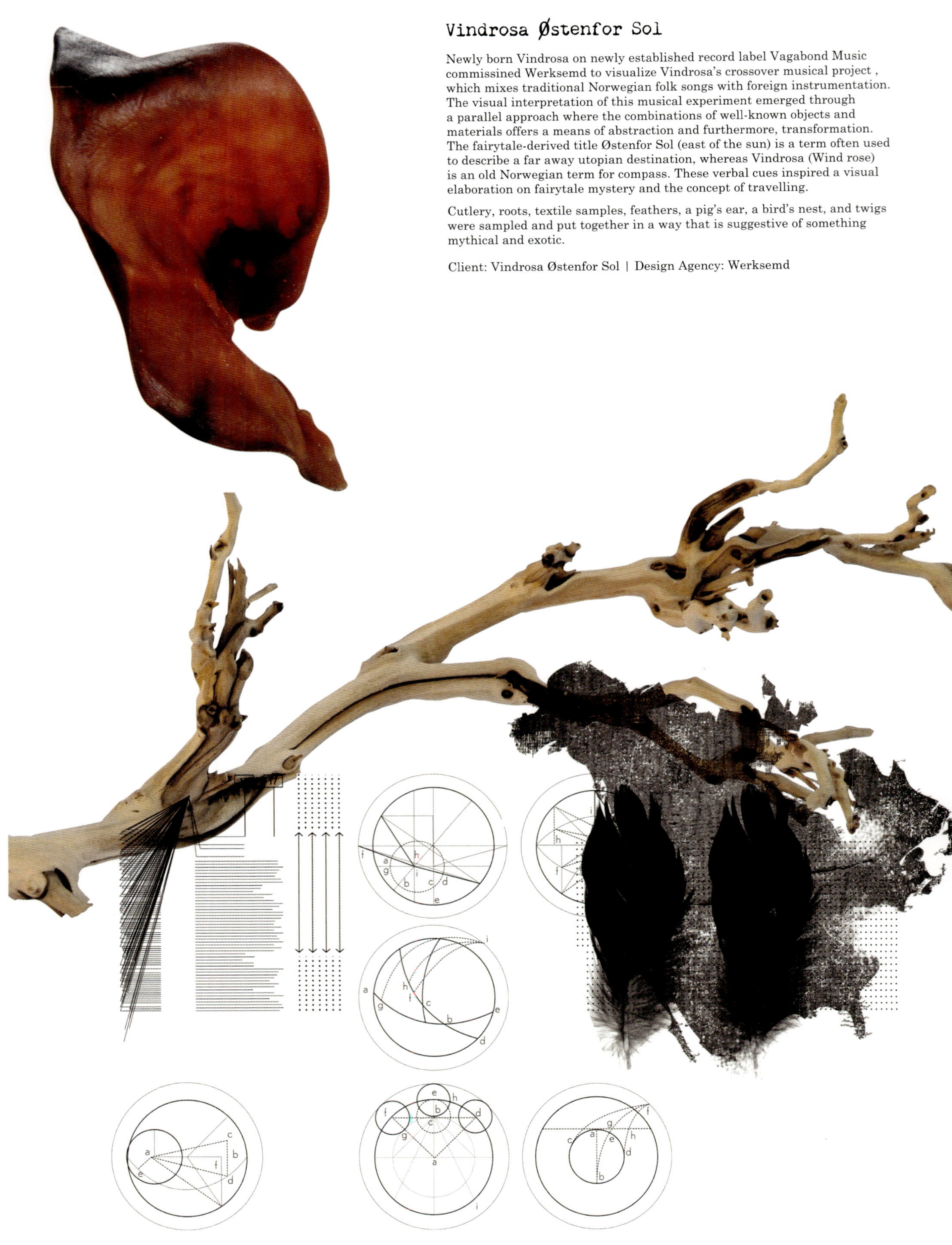

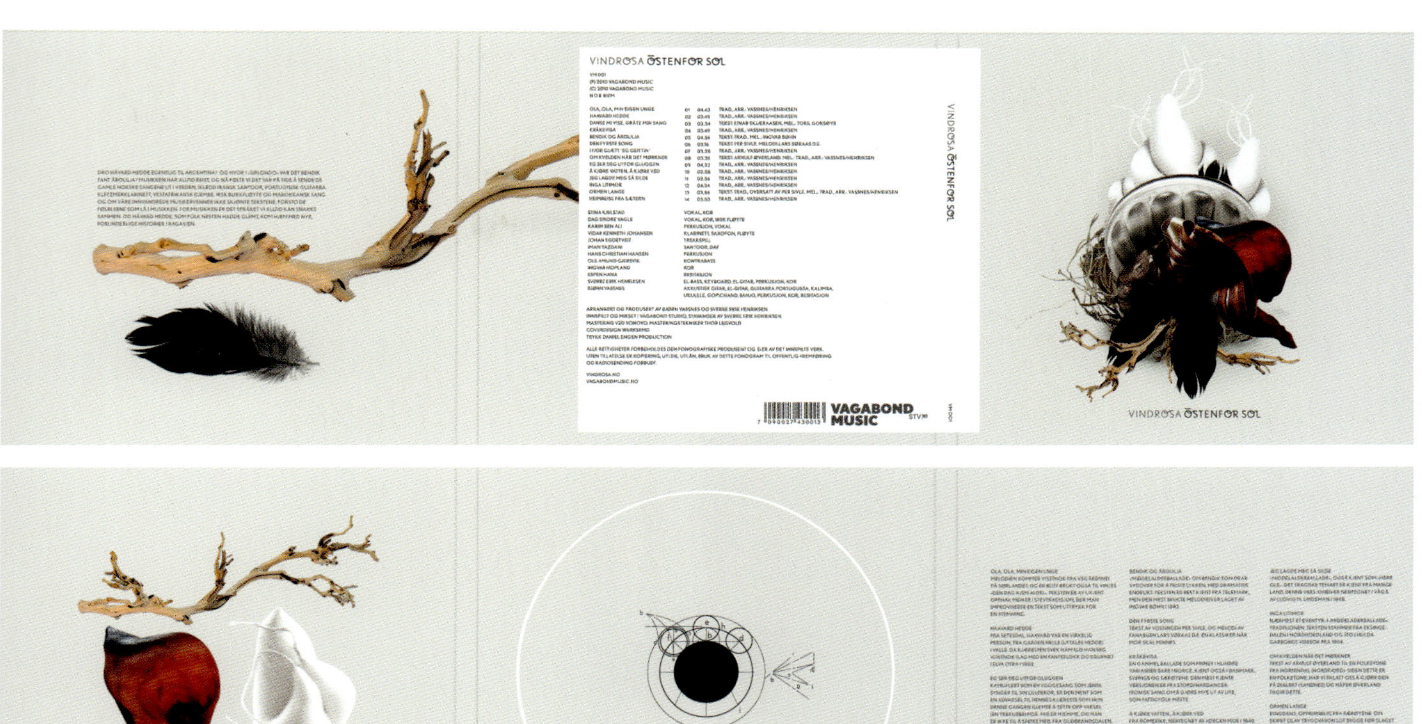

Strand College

Strand College is a school that offers practical and theoretical studies in addition to programs for students with special challenges. As such, it has committed to a philosophy pertaining to the effort of cultivating the potential of each individual student. Strand approached Werksemd with the challenge of developing a visual identity that would reflect their set of values.

The principle is thus translated into all levels of the identity, graphically, illustration-wise, text-wise, and also ruling how editorial content is being organized. The logo itself consists of a split circle that forms the shape of an S, in an ever shifting combination of contrasting colors, textures, and imagery. The relatively free and multifaceted look also expresses Strand's focus on individuality and variety, and is intended to convey a warm and human feel.

Client: Strand College | Design Agency: Werksemd | Design: Nina Elisabeth Børke

ERIK DANIELSEN
REKTOR
TLF 928 52 381
ERIK@STRAND-VGS.NO
STRAND VGS
TORGERKROSSEN
4120 TOU
STRAND VGS
STRAND VGS

WupWup

These are some of Viktor Matics' last flyer and poster designs for "wupwup," an international artist collective, and fashion and music label co-founded by himself. The artworks are developed from with different internet media and based on a twisted look on todays digital zeitgeist. Artworks were part of the exhibition Pancrama 2013 – Festival International de l'Affiche et du Graphisme de Chaumont, France.

Client: WupWup | Design: Viktor Matic

TANZEN IST AUCH SPORT.
KO
NG
WWW.KKOONNGG.COM
PRIELMAYERSTRASSE 6, 80335 MUNICH
WWW.WUPWUP.COM
WWW.TANZEN-IST-AUCH-SPORT.COM
FAMILY AFFAIRS SATURDAY
20·10·12
DREI FARBEN HOUSE & ALEX BAYER

15·DEC·12
SHARON SCHAEL + OLIVER BARDUHN + DAVID GOLDBERG
TANZEN IST AUCH SPORT.
KO
NG

WupWup
SALON
Zur wilden Renate
TANZEN IST AUCH SPORT.
SAMSTAG
14·07·12
RENATE: TANZEN IST AUCH SPORT.

FAMILY AFFAIRS
15·09·12
DEEP DOWN DAVE & FLOORIST
TANZEN IST AUCH SPORT.
KO
NG
WupWup

5
COMBO 11/07
GUSTAVO MM &
MARCIO VERMELHO
THE TWELVES
69
Rua Farme de Amoedo 50
R$40 c/este 15

5
COMBO 02/05
NEPAL
MARCIO VERMELHO
GUI LOPES
69
Rua Farme de Amoedo 50
Favor levar sua identidade
R$30 c/este 15

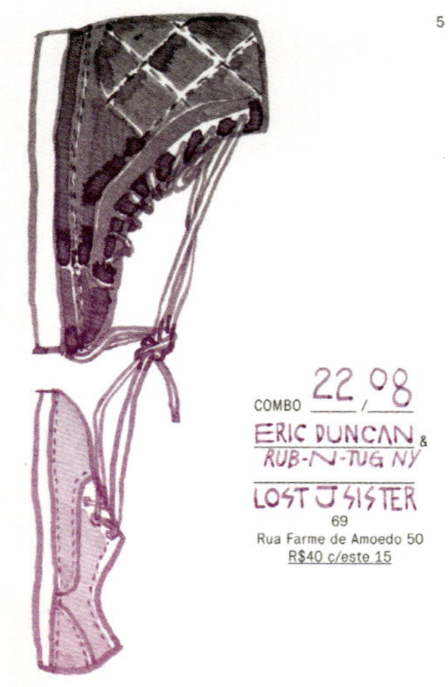
5
COMBO 22/08
ERIC DUNCAN &
RUB-N-TUG NY
LOST & SISTER
69
Rua Farme de Amoedo 50
R$40 c/este 15

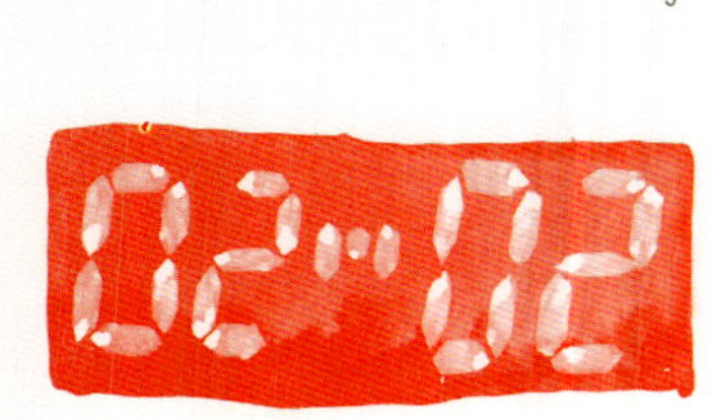
5
02 02
COMBO 30/05
BADENOV &
ASAD RISVI UK
SPARK
69
Rua Farme de Amoedo 50
R$30 c/este 15

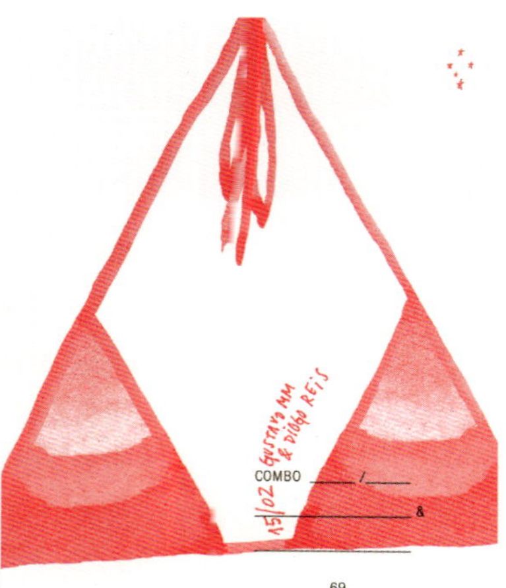
COMBO 15/02
Gustavo MM & Diogo Reis
69
Rua Farme de Amoedo 50
Favor levar sua identidade
Produção: Alexandre Ostrovsky,
Gustavo MM e Daniel Di Salvo
Hostess: Priscila Lima

5
COMBO 04/01
FILIPE (MUSTACHE DJ'S) &
SERGE
69
Rua Farme de Amoedo 50
Favor levar sua identidade
Produção: Alexandre Ostrovsky,
Gustavo MM e Daniel Di Salvo
Hostess: Priscila Lima

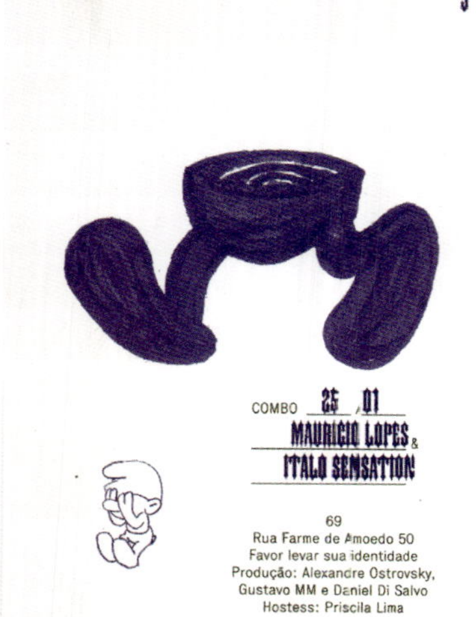
5
COMBO 25/01
MAURICIO LOPES &
ITALO SENSATION
69
Rua Farme de Amoedo 50
Favor levar sua identidade
Produção: Alexandre Ostrovsky,
Gustavo MM e Daniel Di Salvo
Hostess: Priscila Lima

5
COMBO 20/06
WOOLFY DFA/UK
RAFAEL RM2 MEMO &
FILIPE MUSTACHE CALZONE
69
Rua Farme de Amoedo 50
R$30 c/este 15

5
COMBO 16/05
WOMAN AND WOMAN AND WOMAN (SP) &
GUSTAVO MM / BADENOV
69
Rua Farme de Amoedo 50
Favor levar sua identidade
R$30 c/este 15

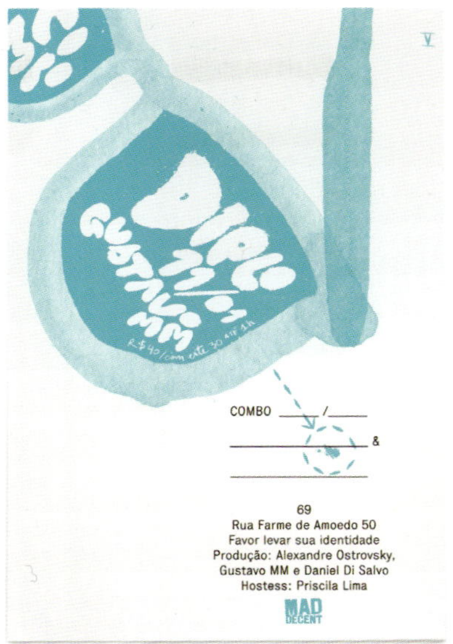

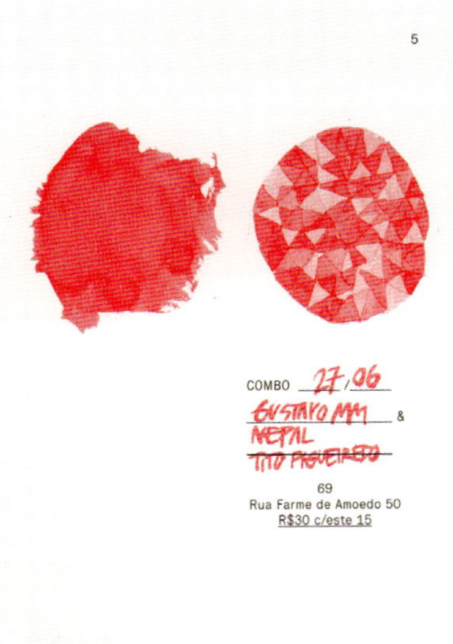

Combo

First year flyers for the Combo party in Rio de Janeiro, Brazil. As the party happens weekly, a template with the recurring information comes in handy.

Client: Combo | Design Agency: Quinta-feira

PACT

PACT is an open space where partnerships between like-minded businesses are housed. The clients' different backgrounds in hairstyling, food, and fashion, challenged the agency to create distinction amidst homogenising the brand experience. PACT first went about designing a unifying element with the use of the ampersand (&) symbol, altering its structure to spell "PACT."

The ampersand celebrates partnerships and is positive about the likelihood of future collaborations. The design execution of marbling was chosen to depict three dissimilar businesses coming together to form a single-minded entity. The swirl and mix of marbling underlines the brand's reflexive yet determined vision of celebrating partnerships.

Client: PACT | Design Agency: ACRE | Creative Direction: T Y Zheng, Jason Song | Design: T Y Zheng

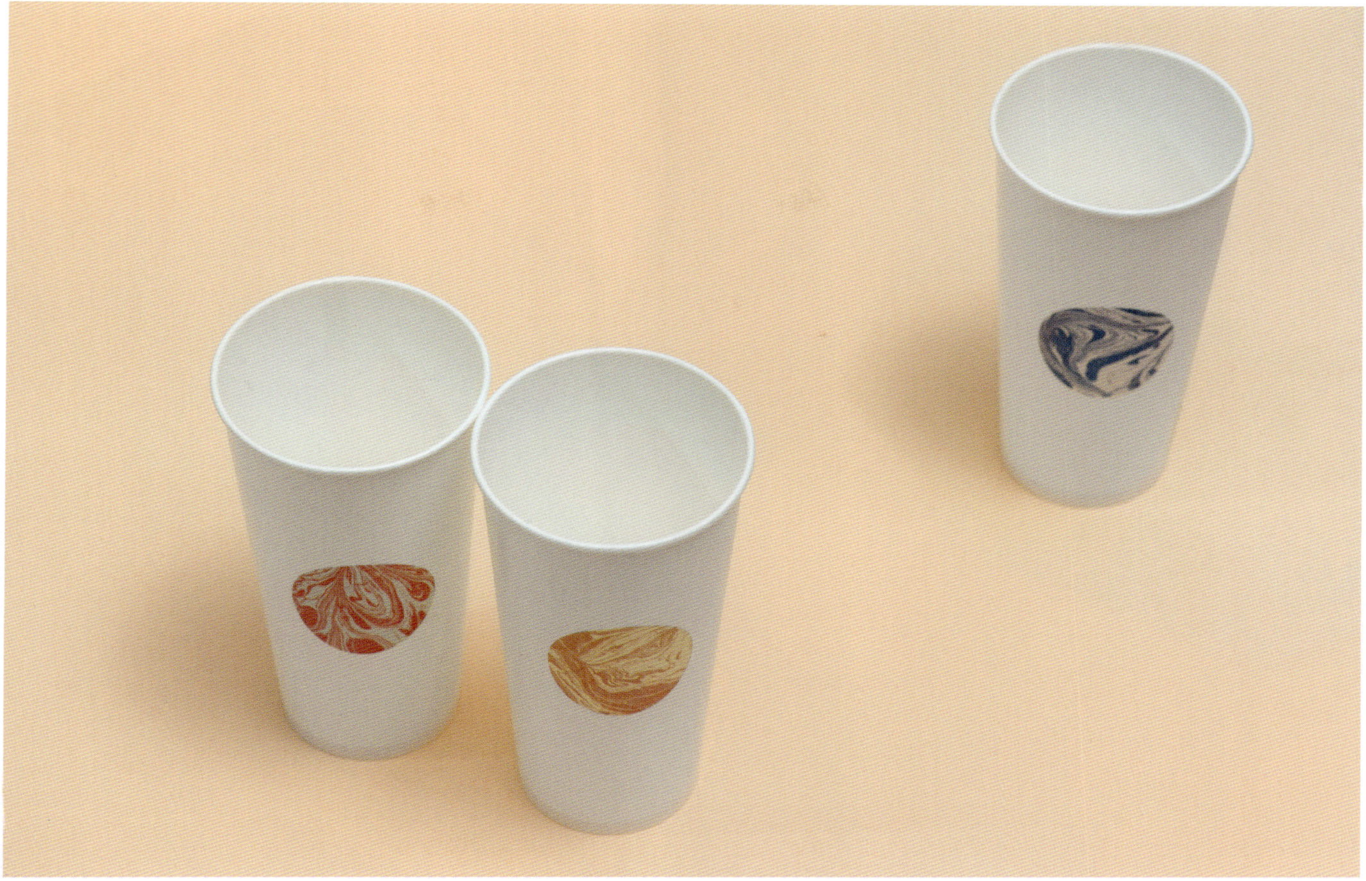

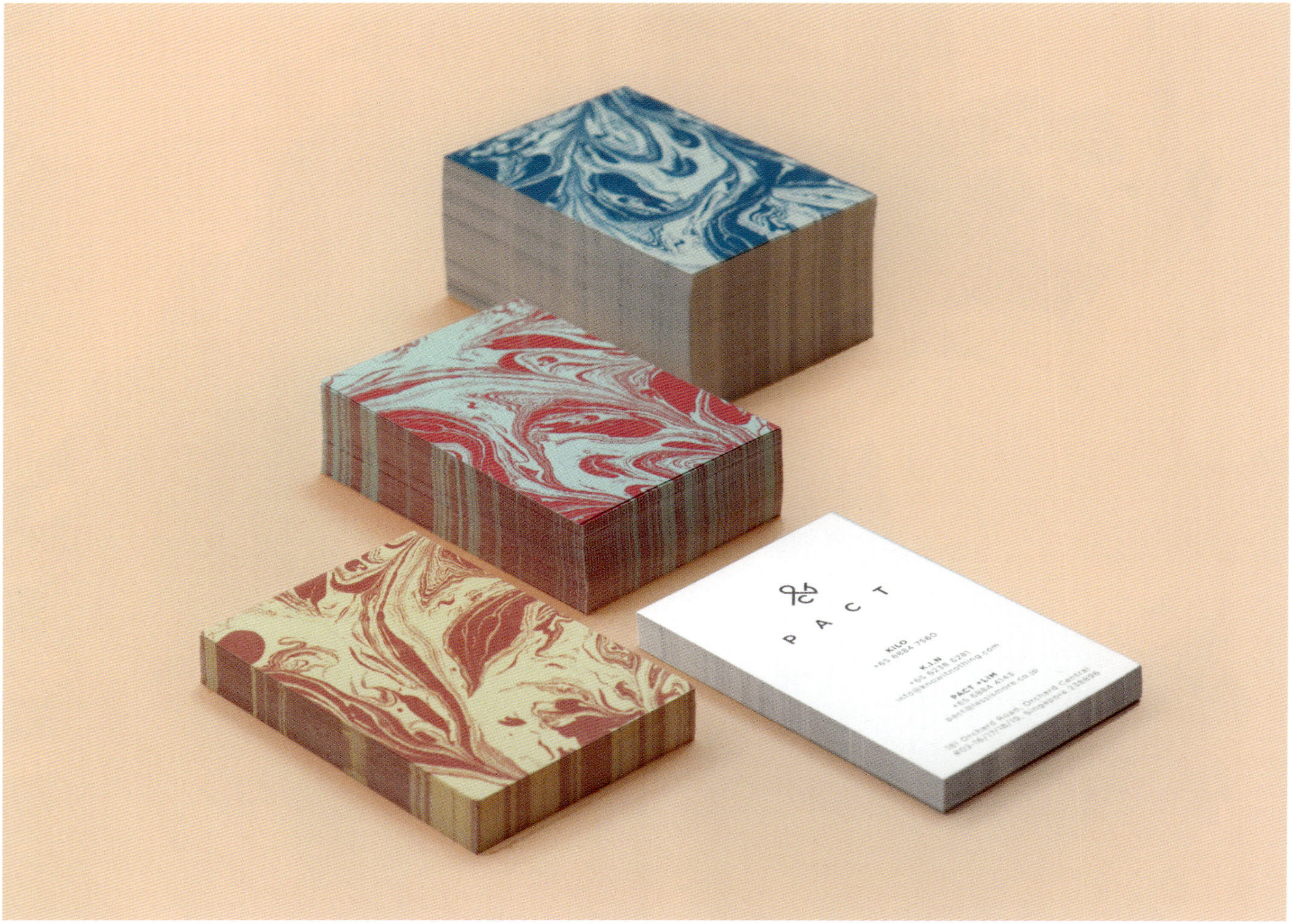
P A C T
KILO
+65 6884 7560
K.I.M
+65 6238 6281

Hello

People move quickly in Hong Kong, living without culture and memory. Meaningful histories and objects gradually disappear without notice. Where did they go? The answer is Hell!

THINGSIDID & ALONGLONGTIME wanted to work on a project that showcase with their skills and creativity, they wanted to resurrect the meaningful histories of objects that had been sent to hell, and bring them back to the public. They wanted to let them say "Hello" again.

This is first project created by Hello. THINGSIDID & ALONGLONGTIME collected a number of old stationery pencils, rulers, and stamps etc. They gave them a new identity and repackaged them using a laser cut printing technique, and brought them back to the public.

Client: Hello | Design Agency: THINGSIDID & ALONGLONGTIME | Design: Jeffrey Tam, Kevin Ng

hell
I AM A
WHITE GLUE
木工用·白膠漿一支

Bonnard

Bonnard is a Mexican French-inspired tea and confectionary shop. The brand's distinct brush strokes and color selection are based on Pierre Bonnard's Post-Impressionist paintings. The simple art direction, together with French words and phonetics, round up the brand's gallic concept effortlessly, spontaneously, and efficiently. Anagrama's approach with clean, sans-serif typography gives Bonnard a luxurious feel usually associated with high-end fashion brands. The gold foil stamp and clean type directly contrasts, and at the same time elevates, the would-be informal paint marks. The rounded cross icon detail found in the wording relates to the shapes of macaroons, one of Bonnard's prime delicacies.

Client: Bonnard | Design Agency: Anagrama

PÂTISSERIE
(À BIENTÔT)
—
BÔNNARD
BÔUTIQUE DE REPÔSTERÍA Y TÉ
EST. 2011
MACARÔNS
(À BIENTÔT)
—
BÔNNARD
BÔUTIQUE DE REPÔSTERÍA Y TÉ
EST. 2011
MACARÔNS
(À BIENTÔT)
—
BÔNNARD
BÔUTIQUE DE REPÔSTERÍA Y TÉ

The Curators Conference

Launched in September 2012, The Curators Conference provides a unique opportunity for discussion around the theme of curation, featuring speakers from a variety of creative fields. RoAndCo' s branding for the conference included tote bags, programs, posters, web design and art direction. Inspired by curation and process, they deliberately used a stark black-and-white palette in the weeks leading up to the conference; the day it began, the event literally "came to life" with the introduction of color throughout all its collateral. Using watercolor effects, several colors bled across the branding elements, evoking the idea of boundless creative expression and how contemporary curation influences disciplines from art to design, fashion and technology.

Client: Portable | Design Agency: RoAndCo | Creative Direction: Roanne Adams | Art Direction: Roanne Adams | Copywriter: n/a | Illustration: n/a | Photography: n/a

09.05
CURATORS
CONFERENCE
NEW YORK
2012

09.05
CURATORS
CONFERENCE
NEW YORK
2012
SCHEDULE
C/C

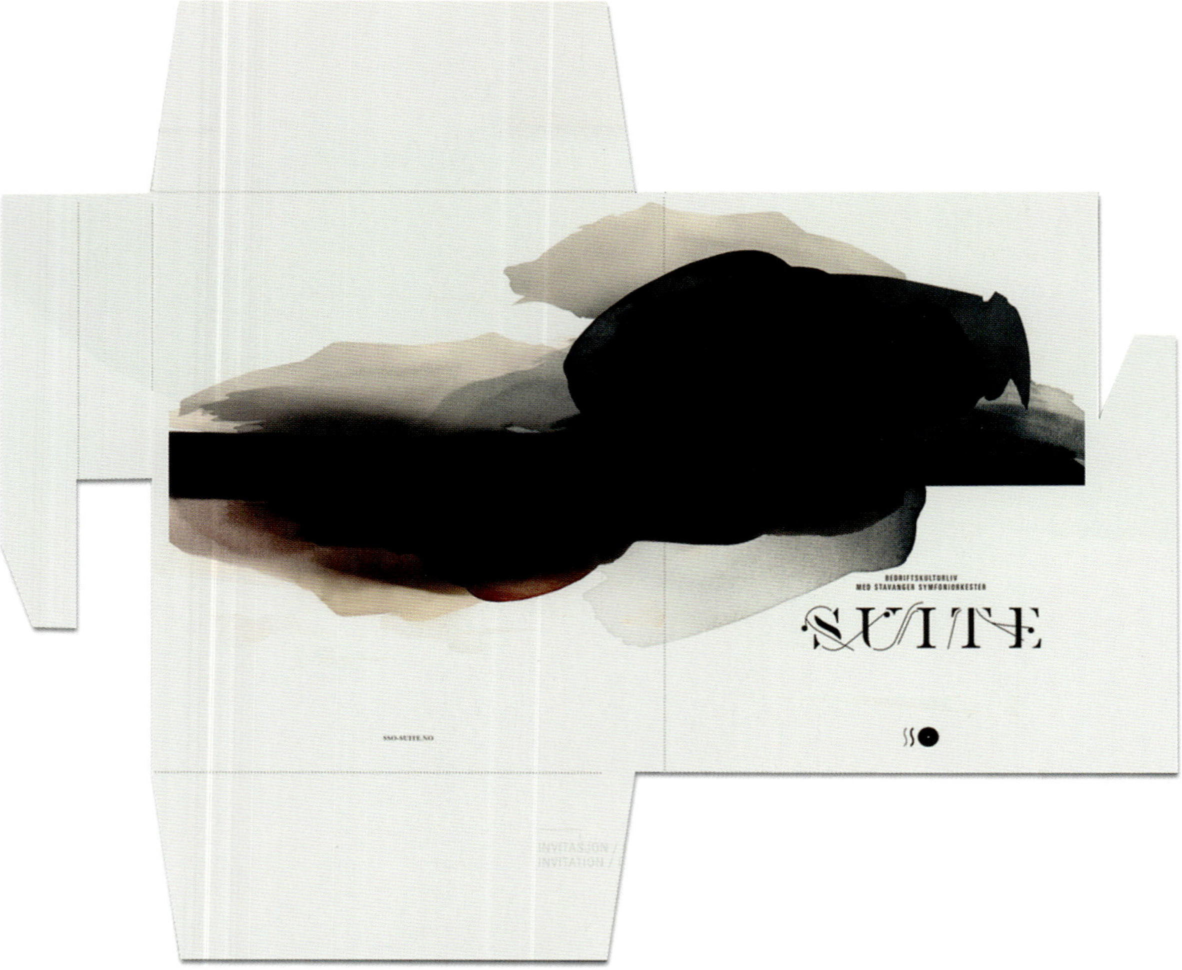

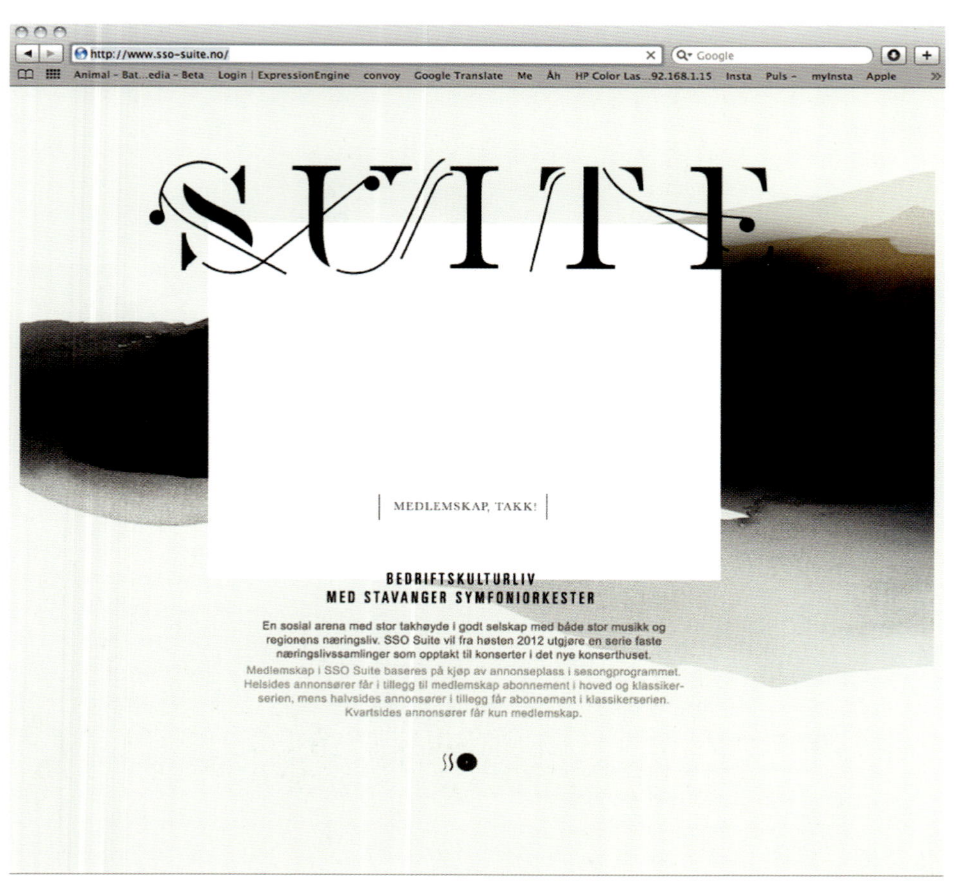
http://www.sso-suite.no/
SUITE
MEDLEMSKAP, TAKK!
BEDRIFTSKULTURLIV
MED STAVANGER SYMFONIORKESTER
En sosial arena med stor takhøyde i godt selskap med både stor musikk og regionens næringsliv. SSO Suite vil fra høsten 2012 utgjøre en serie faste næringslivssamlinger som opptakt til konserter i det nye konserthuset.
Medlemskap i SSO Suite baseres på kjøp av annonseplass i sesongprogrammet. Helsides annonsører får i tillegg til medlemskap abonnement i hoved og klassiker-serien, mens halvsides annonsører i tillegg får abonnement i klassikerserien. Kvartsides annonsører får kun medlemskap.

SSO Suite

Artwork and graphic profile for the Stavanger Symphonic Orchestra Society Suite.

Client: SSO Suite | Design Agency: Werksemd

Arboris

The task was to develop the concept for a premium brand of organic skin care cosmetics. To offer innovative solutions, eyeing, in particular, the European market. The name Arboris (in Latin – "tree") appears on the base of the completely natural composition, which includes nothing but vegetable ingredients. Arboris products, due to their natural origin, have a small shelf life. Ohmybrand proposed to use a special paint in the design of the labels. The paint begins to fade when the cream loses its freshness. The black color and mascara-stylized appearance show the premium qualities of the product, and make it stand out from the mass of skin care cosmetics.

Client: Arboris | Design Agency: Ohmybrand | Creative Direction: Nadie Parshina | Illustranion: Nadie Parshina | Copywriter: Svetlana Chugunova

Arboris
ORGANIC COSMETICS
FACIAL
TONER
Arboris
FACIAL
TONER

Arboris
ORGANIC COSMETICS
DAY
EMULSION
Arboris
ORGANIC COSMETICS
PROTECTIVE
DAY CREAM
Arboris
ANTI-AGING EYE CREAM

Laura Díaz

As unique as the creations in her kitchen, Laura Díaz Catering came to us with a simple, yet original idea: classic typewriter font with black and white illustrations. La Tortillería wanted to bring her business to life, so they decided to take it to the next level by keeping this premise, and adding some color to her image. They included illustrations full of movement and detail to pique her clients' interest and inspire them to try her out. Her objective: to create good memories and flavors that will last a lifetime. La Tortillería's: to give her business a fresh personality and an eye catching website to reflect her professionalism, and her passion. They produced the reinvention of a business that will keep on giving for years to come. The final delivery included a new logo, a full website redesign, business cards, place cards, stationery, and packaging materials that definitely take the cake!

Client: Laura Díaz Catering | Design Agency: La Tortillería

LAURA DIAZ
catering

DULCE SALADO PASTEL BLANCO GOURMET CONTACTO

Crepas

Pollo en salsita roja, en crema de chile poblano con elote y queso.
Pollo en salsita roja, en salsa verde y un toque de picante.
Pollo en salsita verde, en salsa de cilantro a gratín.
Flor de calabaza y elote, en salsa cremosa blanca.
Espinacas a la crema, en salsa roja de la casa con elote y al gratín.

Se recomiendan 3-4 por persona.
-

Quiche (pay)

Jamón y tres quesos.
Espinacas a la crema con queso y un poco de tocino crujiente.
Queso amarillo y brócoli con un toque de piñones.
Rajas con queso blanco y elote.
Espárragos a los tres quesos.

Cada pay es para 8 px.
Quiches tamaño personal disponibles.
-

Pannini / Muffin salado / Bagel

Crema fresca al eneldo, con salmón ahumado y un toque de limón. Pieza.
Jamón y quesos. Pieza.
Huevos benedictos. (Desayuno clásico). Pieza.
Crema dulce con chutney de frutas (mermelada de la casa).
-

Empanadas rellenas

Jamón y queso al piquillo.
Rajas con queso y elote.
Huitlacoche a la crema.
Espinacas a la crema con elote.
-

COPYRIGHT © 2011 - DESIGN BY LA TORTILLERIA

1979

1979 is a restaurant situated in the 1st arrondissement of Paris. While promoting their restaurant, they also wanted to develop their club, and increase its visibility. FLOZ created the visual identity of 1979's club by working on the graphic charter without touching the logo.

FLOZ also designed the presentation of flyers, programs, graphic elements used in the charter, the newsletter, events photo reports, and finally the menu of the restaurant.

Client: 1979 | Design Agency: FLOZ

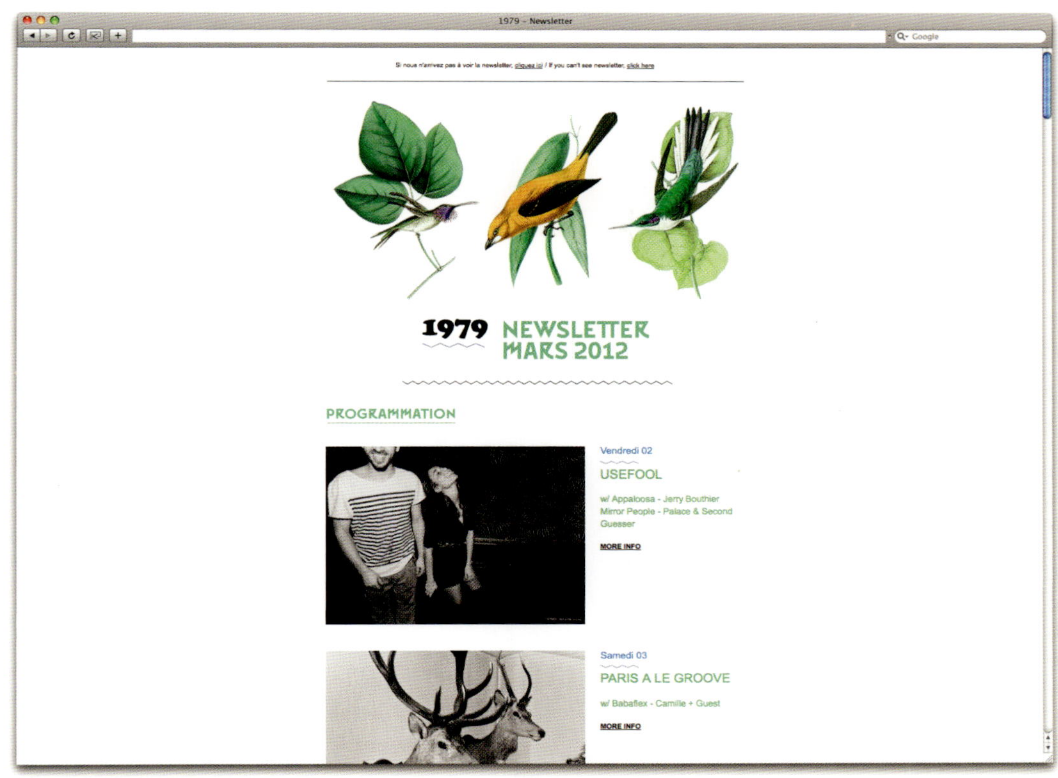
1979 - Newsletter
1979 NEWSLETTER
MARS 2012
PROGRAMMATION
Vendredi 02
USEFOOL
w/ Appaloosa - Jerry Bouthier
Mirror People - Palace & Second Guesser
MORE INFO
Samedi 03
PARIS A LE GROOVE
w/ Babaflex - Camille + Guest
MORE INFO

1979
PROGRAMMATION
MARS 2012
Vendredi 02
USEFOOL
w/ Appaloosa - Jerry Bouthier
Mirror People - Palace & Second Guesser
Samedi 03
PARIS A LE GROOVE
w/ Babaflex - Camille + Guest
Vendredi 09
PREMIER RENDEZ VOUS
w/ Olaf Hvnd (live) - Dj Tcheck
L'Horloger - Othello - Blondon
Aurèle MC - Dj Tom-K
Jeudi 15
BURLESQUE KLUB
w/ Elodelu - Mlle Joris
Mimi de Montmartre - Miss Glitter Painkiller
Valentina Del Pearls
Vendredi 16
LES GARÇONS
EN CULOTTE COURTE
w/ Dj Little Nemo + Guest
Samedi 17
1979
2 ANS!
w/ Walter Wallace - Camille
Stéphane Bourbon - Julielarule & Nightlife
AB'L - Clément (Colette) - Real Abstract
T-Dogg - Dee Nice
Vendredi 23
MEEX THEORY
w/ Twoda & Walter Wallace
Samedi 24
PRIVATISATION
Vendredi 30
DRINKS PARTY
w/ Dj Alec - Hush Hush
Samedi 31
PARIS A LE GROOVE
w/ Babaflex - Camille + Guest

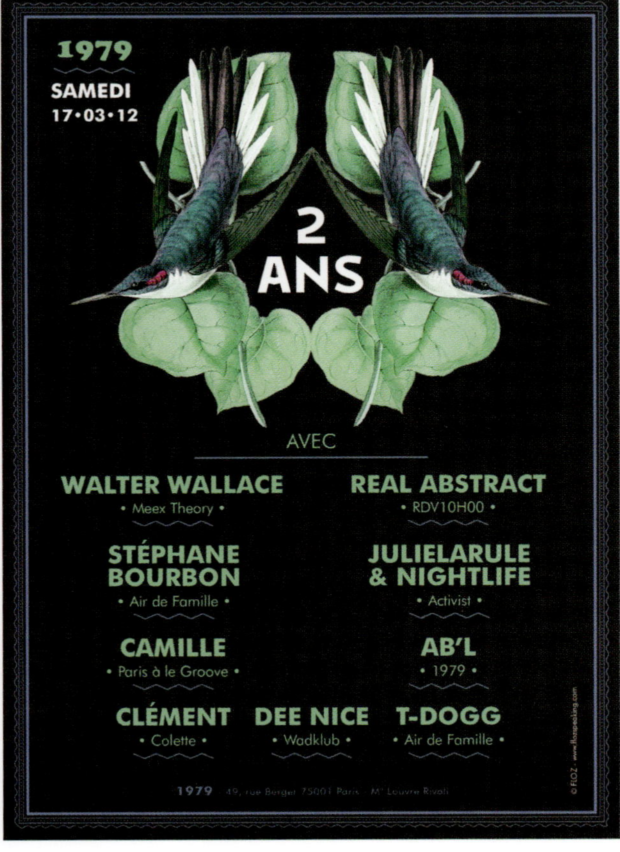
1979
SAMEDI
17•03•12
2
ANS
AVEC
WALTER WALLACE
• Meex Theory •
REAL ABSTRACT
• RDV10H00 •
STÉPHANE
BOURBON
• Air de Famille •
JULIELARULE
& NIGHTLIFE
• Activist •
CAMILLE
• Paris à le Groove •
AB'L
• 1979 •
CLÉMENT
• Colette •
DEE NICE
• Wadklub •
T-DOGG
• Air de Famille •

Coccogelo

Coccogelo prides itself on its inventive high quality gelato. To express this key message, 5 characters were created and sent on expeditions through wild and treacherous landscapes in search of inspirations for creative new flavors. These quirky characters were illustrated and their stories translated across various collaterals.

Client: Coccogelo | Design Agency: Somewhere Else | Illustration: Messymsxi | Photography: Felix Lee

High Shoulders

Lady Fozaza's jackets are created with her signature "High Shoulders." The advertisements show the effect of these high shoulders on the shoulder pets.

Client: Lady Fozaza | Design Agency: Livingroom Communication, UAE | Creative Direction: Martino O'Brien, Mansoor A. Bhatti | Art Direction: Jana Jelovac, Lara Bizri, Nisreen Shahin, Mansoor A. Bhatti | Illustration: Jana Jelovac | Copywriter: Sarah Berro

Lady FOZAZA
HIGH
SHOULDERS

Shapeshift

Shapeshift is a multidisciplinary, thematic entity, consisting of three independent exhibitions: “Isolation,” “This Image is No More,” and “Interiors.” The people behind the projects are Finnish, and international artists from the fields of theater, music, narrative art, dance, poetry, and fine art. Shapeshift’s aim is to conduct critical social discussions, bring together the creators and the viewers of art, and involve the residents of Helsinki. The visual identity evolved from the concept of seeing, hearing, and speaking into an Escher-like transformation from the eye to the lips.

Client: Gallery Sinne | Design Agency: Tsto | Art Direction: Jaakko Pietiläinen, Tsto

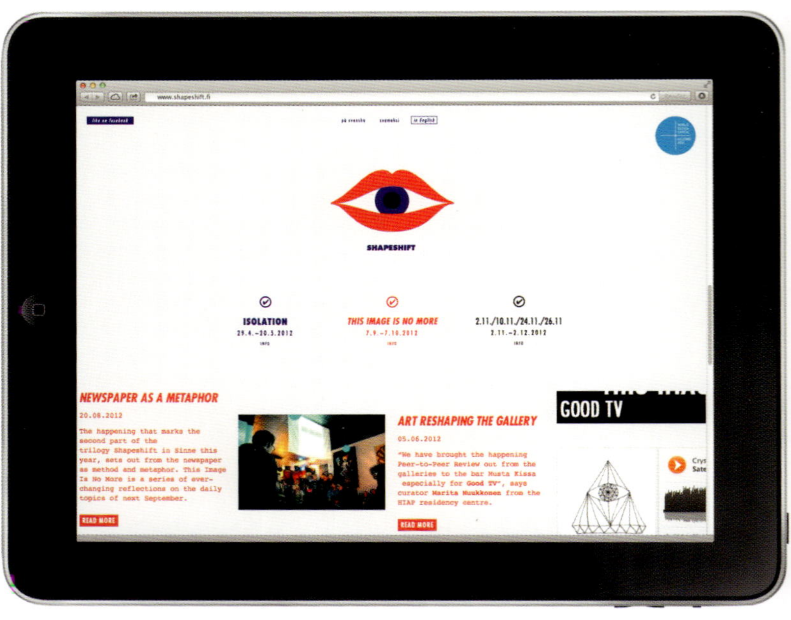

World Design Capital Helsinki 2012 Products

The World Design Capital Helsinki 2012 initiative celebrated openness by taking citizens to the center of the visual identity process, and asked them to create a symbol or graphic for a world capital of design. This was done through multiple workshops executed as open platforms for experimentation and participation for all people. In parallel with this nonprofessional approach, established designers were invited to join in the creation of official WDC Helsinki 2012 products. The same brief that was given to people at Open Identity workshops was presented to a group of Finnish designers – including architects, graphic designers, industrial designers, and textile designers such as Vuokko Nurmesniemi, Kustaa Saksi, Oiva Toikka, and Tuomas Toivonen. A collection of products ranging from clothing to various accessories featured the final artworks by group members. Alongside this “pro collection” a series of products were created celebrating the general public's work as well. These included various collectibles for home – and especially for children’s rooms.

Client: World Design Capital Helsinki 2012 | Design Agency: Kokoro & Moi

Vårdapoteket

Vårdapoteket is a Swedish pharmacy chain with 24 pharmacies placed in care related locations. To distinguish and contrast themselves from the often clinical and barren environments that hospitals comprise, SDL developed a new identity inspired by the human body. With a strong and positive color palette, and a pattern based on the internal organs of the human body, a strong base for their new identity was created. This graphic language is now used in all types of applications; from in-store wallpaper to all sorts of printed material such as stationery, retail, and POS materials. We provided Vårdapoteket with a simple and playful toolbox that creates an inspiring identity, and much appreciated retail environment.

Client: Vårdapoteket | Design Agency: Stockholm Design Lab | Creative Direction: Björn Kusoffsky | Art Direction: Nina Granath | Design: Lisa Fleck | Illustration: Kari Moden | Photography: Felix Odell

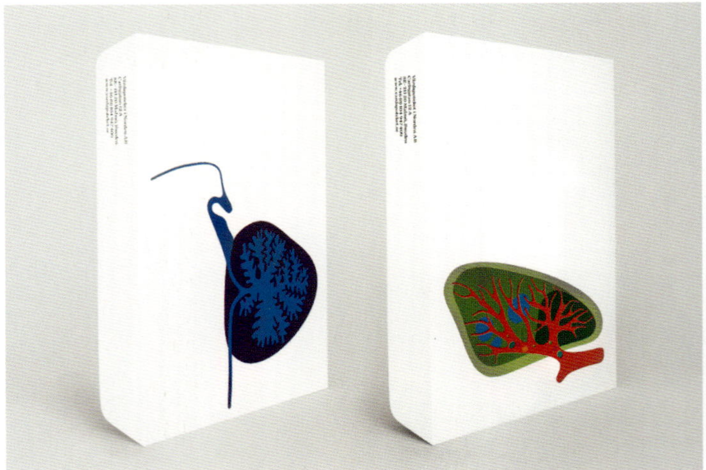

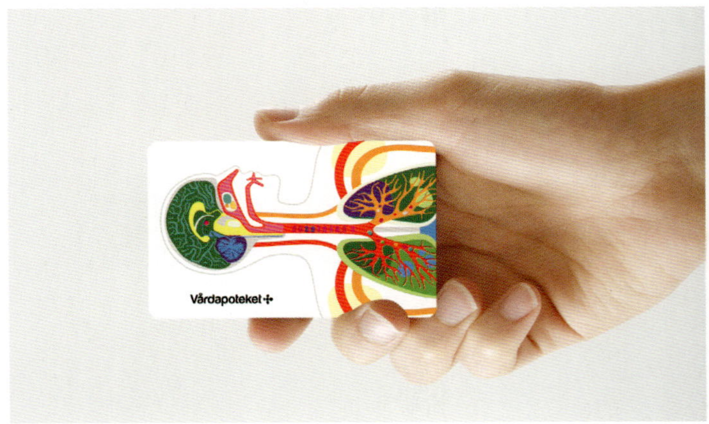

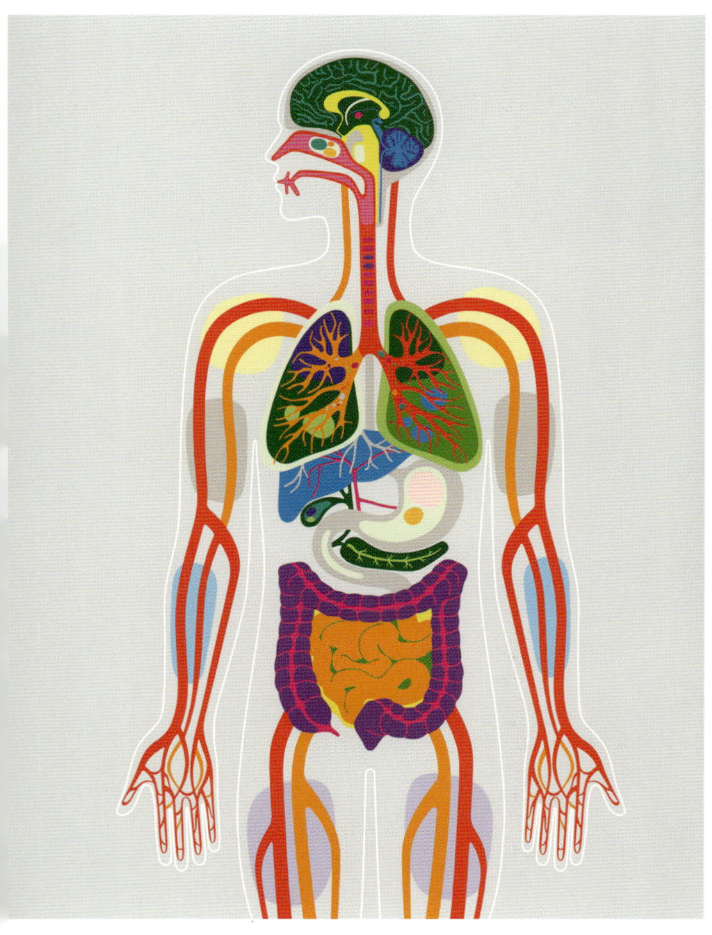

NÄRA VÅRDEN har gjort oss OVANLIGT DUKTIGA på
MEDEL. Vi har dessutom ovanligt MÅNGA på lager. På vårt apotek
MÄNNISKOR med VARIERANDE BEHOV. Det märker du
FRISK OAS här på sjukhuset.
UPPLEVA det idag!
dig.

Slowly by Da Dolce

Like a clear stream in a desert, there is a small trendy design center in the basement of a bustling shopping center. Embraced in a white space, there is an open cafe that combines bookstore, gelato, and Internet radio studio in one place. United by different elements in a peaceful design, a kind of "LOHAS" culture is formed.

Client: Da Dolce Limited | Design Agency: Tommy Li Design Workshop Ltd. | Creative Direction: Tommy Li | Design: Renatus Wu

Slow is the rebellion against banal efficiency. Revealed. Resurrected. Anti-traffic. Moments refined by discovering the invisible. Love organic food, eat to fulfil but not to fill. Chat, friends and foes! Slow knows no borders. Smell your coffee, and your magazine on the rack, as music hums into your ears. Slow is our life, at least, for once.

SHOP 26 & 27 ON BASEMENT 2, LANGHAM PLACE, 8 ARGYLE STREET, MONGKOK, KOWLOON / 九龍旺角亞皆老街8號朗豪坊地庫B2層26及27號舖
TEL & FAX : +852 2377 1557 / 11:00 to 23:00

SLOWLY
BY DA DOLCE

Designed by
Tommy Li Design
Workshop

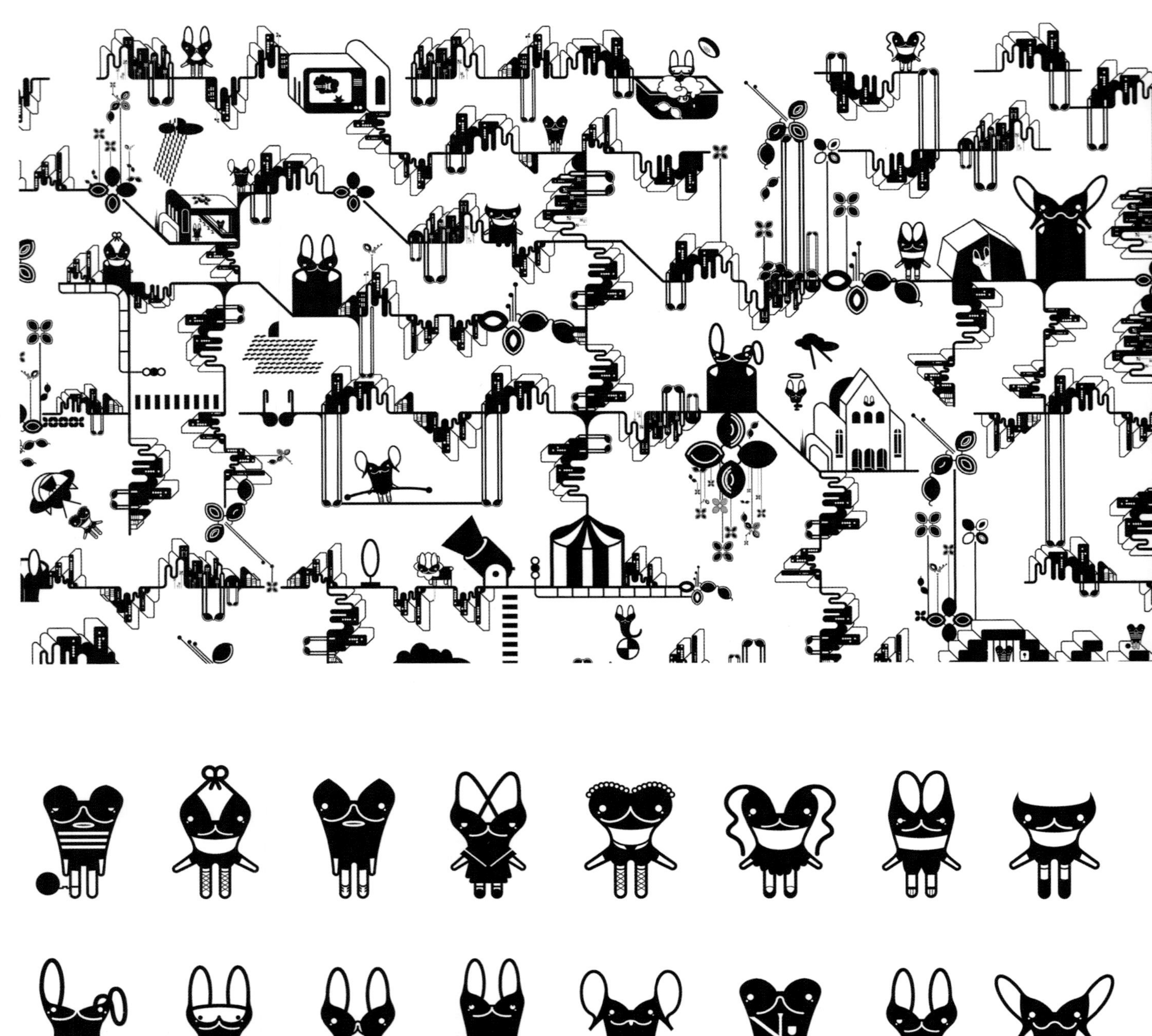

Blablabra

In order to rejuvenate an old-fashioned lingerie brand into a brand for young girls, Tommy Li Design had to begin by looking at the way the target customers live. Creating a creative and dynamic "bra city" with different bra characters who represent different personalities, they portrayed the ideas of heaven and hell in a metropolitan city. It is this kind of black humor that the agency wanted to play on, and breakthrough from an out-of-date lingerie brand and become a fresh concept where teenage girls could feel like they belonged. Since lingerie is something private for young girls, the brand name helps them disguise their little secret – "bla bla bra ..."

Client: Godsend Trading Co., Ltd | Design Agency: Tommy Li Design Workshop Ltd. | Creative Direction: Tommy Li | Art Direction: Thomas Siu

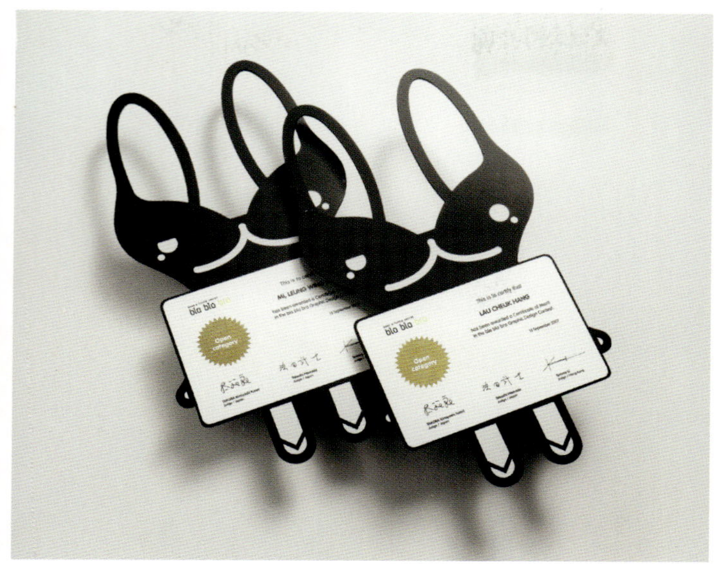

keep a little secret
bla bla bra

keep a little secret
bla bla bra
Katie Lam
Graphic Designer
4/F., M.Bux Tower, 119 Wo Yi Hop Rd.,
Kwai Chung, Hong Kong
T : (852) 2614 5078
F : (852) 2614 4711
E : godsend@hkstar.com
Godsend Trading Co., Ltd.
(A subsidiary of Tinko Pacific Group)

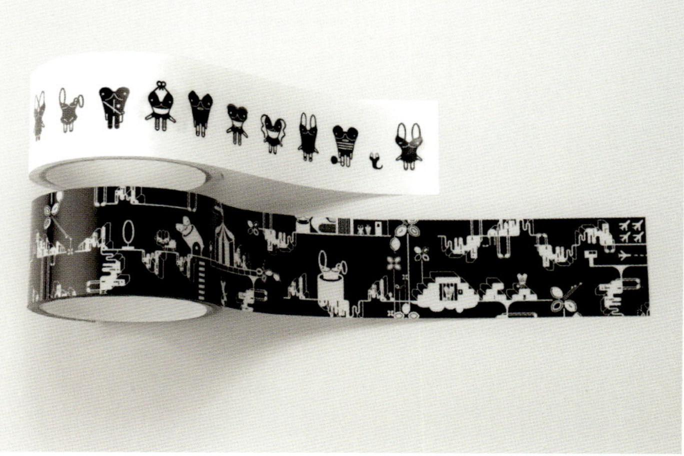

Brokula&Ž

Brokula&Ž (Broccoli&Z) is a clothing brand made of organically grown raw materials. With Brokula&Ž, everything good comes from within, so all the clothing contains hidden messages written on the inside that can be seen only by you … and whoever undresses you. The messages are funny dialog between Brokula (Broccoli) and Z (a bird). The packaging had to be as eco-friendly as possible, but also fun. The inks have ecological certificates, and the paper is recycled. It's designed as a cup that you can use for something else after unpacking your purchase. It's easy to assemble without any glue or plastic.

Client: Brokula&Ž | Design Agency: Bruketa&Žinić OM | Creative Direction: Davor Bruketa, Nikola Zinic | Art Direction: Nebojsa Cvetkovic | Design: Nebojsa Cvetkovic | Copywriter: Ivan Cadez | Illustration: Nebojsa Cvetkovic | Photography: Domagoj Kunic

48%
PRIRODNA VLAKNA
IZ PULPE DRVETA/
NATURAL WOOD
PULP FIBERS
4%
ELASTINSKO VLAKNO ZA
TRAJNOST I UDOBNOST
ELASTANE FOR DURA
BILITY & COMFORT

Voli svog
susjeda.
...ali pazi
da te muž
ne uhvati.

BROKULA&Ž
WWW.BROKULAZ.COM
Bitno
uvijek dolazi
iznutra
ECO

Le Nid

Le Nid, the bar Jean Jullien has been working on for a year, has finally opened its doors!

Located in Nantes, France, it sits at the top of a 144m building called Tour de Bretagne and overlooks the city and its surroundings. Inside the bar, a 40 meters long bird rests. The bar is located in its body, whilst his neck runs to the other end of the space, leading you to its massive head. His eyes opens and close regularly, as he falls asleep and wakes up. You can enjoy a drink in his egg shaped tables and chairs. Outside, the terrace offers a 360 degree view with a giant orientation table that runs over 100 meters. Last but not least, Niwouinwouin created a unique soundtrack to finish the identity of Le Nid.

Client: Le Nid | Design: Jean Jullien

de la Beaujoi
PORTERIE
SIMILIEN
FRAC PAYS DE LA LOIRE
COURS DES 50 OTAGES
PONT DE LA TORTIERE
Saint Donatien
Ile de Versailles

LYCÉE CLEMENCEAU

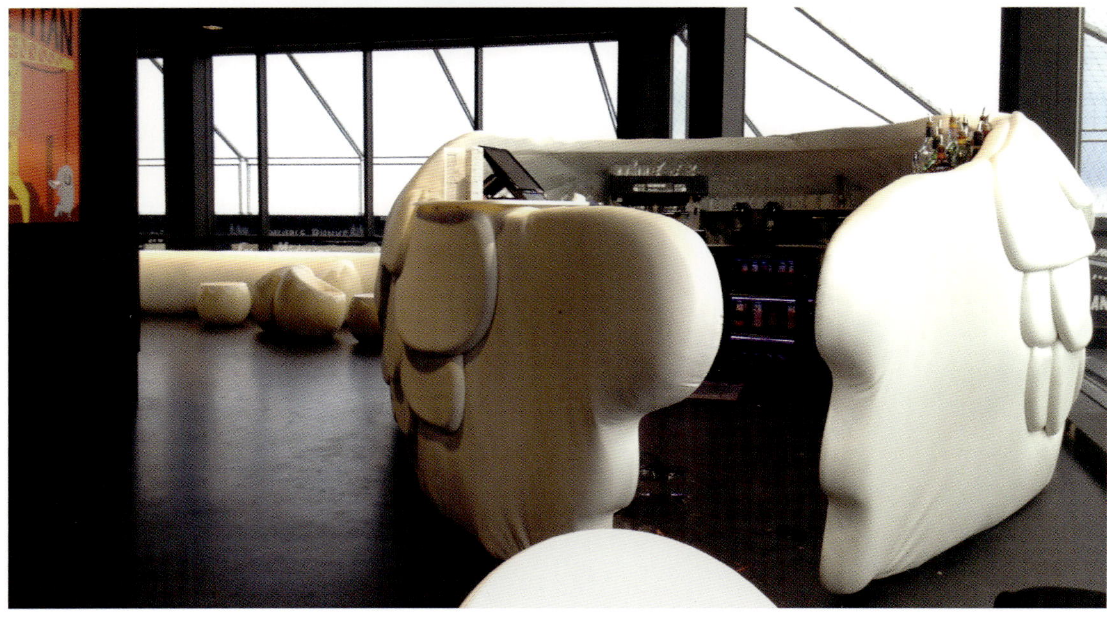

Cowboy Seven

Point–Blank Design Ltd. were asked to develop an identity to redefine the “western cowboy” concept for this drink cafe. Fine details complement the Wild West elements of the new design, which updates the original rough and wild appearance of the cafe.

Client: Delish Brands Management Ltd. | Design Agency: Point-Blank Design Ltd. | Design: Lawrence Choy, Stephen Wong

IT'S HOT CHOCOLATE
WARM HEARTED HOT CHOCOLATE
COWBOY 7 SEVEN
Shop 3133B
3/F Lok Fu Plaza
198 Junction Rd.
Kowloon
+852 26689289

IT'S HOT CHOCOLATE
Forget love,
I'd rather fall
in chocolate.
COWBOY 7 SEVEN

Your Lucky Drinks
FINE CHOCOLATE
COWBOY SEVEN
COFFEE AND TEA
REFRESHING

COWBOY
7
Your Lucky Drinks
SEVEN
TM

Eyescream & Friends

This is a Taiwan-style shaved ice cream (yet made with Italian gelato) with a texture somewhere between sorbet, and ice cream. It's kind of particular, an amorphous mass of ice cream with lots of sauces and toppings falling from above and to the sides. The project was slightly complex because this type of ice is unknown in Europe, from the aesthetic criteria about local food, this ice cream is not very attractive.

Estudio m Barcelona created a creative strategy around this ugliness: starting with a "deconstruction" of the ingredients (packaging-tray with different containers). But the key creative twist was putting two sugar eyes on top of this ice cream mountain, making it a character-monster that looks you in the eyes, and immediately gives it life and personality.

From there, the naming came easily: Eyescream, which in English is pronounced like ice cream.

Client: Joad López, Federico Mendoza | Design Agency: Estudio m Barcelona | Design: Merche Alcalá, Marion Dönneweg | Illustration: Marion Dönneweg | Copywriter: Jorge Virgós | Photography: Daniel Loewe

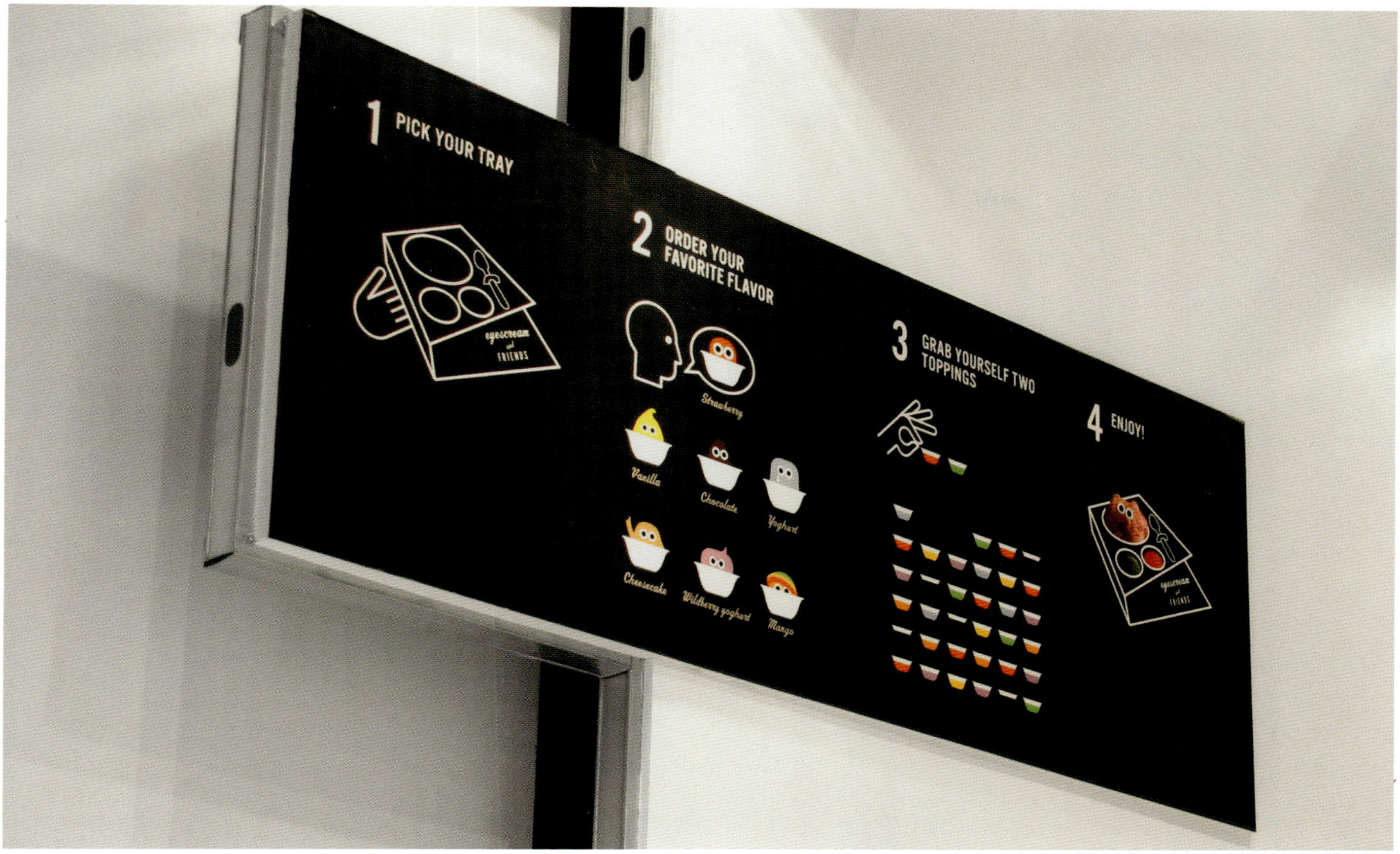

1 PICK YOUR TRAY
2 ORDER YOUR FAVORITE FLAVOR
3 GRAB YOURSELF TWO TOPPINGS
4 ENJOY!
Strawberry
Vanilla
Chocolate
Yoghurt
Cheesecake
Wildberry yoghurt
Mango

Mr. Lonely
Yoghurt
Very Berry
Strawberry
Cheese loves Cake
Cheesecake
Willy Wild
Wildberry yoghurt
Bob Mango
Mango

30
eyescream
and
FRIENDS
Vanilla
Chocolate
Yoghurt
Mango
Coolest ice cream in town!
Strawberry
Wildberry yoghurt
Cheesecake

Das Techno Café

Bureau FFabienne created a new look for the hottest Tuesday summer location in Vienna, Austria: the well-known Das Techno Café, located in the beautiful Pavillon in Volksgarten, Vienna.

Bureau FFabienne designed a new website, flyers, and weekly newsletter. There are 5 different key visuals, which change monthly.

Client: Das Techno Café | Design Agency: Bureau FFabienne | Design: Fabienne Feltus

2012
Mai
das techno cafe
FFABIENNE.COM

2012
Juni
das techno cafe
FFABIENNE.COM

2012
August
das techno cafe
FFABIENNE.COM

2012
Juli
das techno cafe
FFABIENNE.COM

Makisan

The client wanted to launch Singapore's first ever fully customizable sushi store. A wide selection of fresh ingredients are on offer, and diners pick and choose precisely what goes into their hand-rolls. Kinetic Design and Advertising proposed naming the store "Makisan" for one simple reason: the word "san" roughly translates as "mister" or "missus" in Japanese, and by using this suffix, each Maki could be uniquely personified. This idea also extends to operations: customers can name their own rolls however they choose. The logo is made up of emoticons commonly used in Japanese pop culture. Using hand-drawn illustrations of mushrooms, avocados, cucumbers, and other ingredients, they designed a myriad of patterns, which became Makisan's main visual identity. These motifs were applied throughout the consumer experience – right down to the packaging – to play up the endless, fun options available for diners. Vibrant colors were used for the store's interior, creating an energetic atmosphere to attract a chic crowd looking for something more than just average sushi.

Client: Makisan | Design Agency: Kinetic Design and Advertising

Chocolee

Inspired by origami and "furoshiki," Japanese wrapping cloths, "Chocolee" chocolates feature patterns designed with both collaged and digitally drawn food elements. Each square wrapper can be easily repurposed for paper-folding and crafting.

This imaginary chocolate brand emphasizes not only beautiful wrapping, but the fun in its re-use, giving the paper a second life as gift wrap, or even a paper crane. By paying attention to the art of wrapping, we bring moments of aesthetic pleasure and play into everyday life.

Design: Kathy Wu

chocolee
est. 1993
There's a reason our chocolates are so good. It's nothing but the best stuff–Brazilian cacao, organic cane sugar. We believe in unique, artful chocolate, inside and out. We love what we make, and hope you do too.
This paper was made for you, so feel free to reuse it! (For origami ideas, visit chocolee.com)
100 Kaffeeplatz, Providence, RI 02903
978 123 4567
chocolee.com
mmmm.
chocolee.com

100 Kaffeeplatz, Providence, RI 02903
978 123 4567
chocolee.com
chocolee
Unique, artful chocolate.

Baked Global Cookies

Baked Global Sdn. Bhd. is a Malaysian cookie manufacturer. Headed by a young and charismatic owner, they first approached The Composer to create the entire identity along with packaging. They wanted a young, fun, and witty approach for their identity. Along with the creation and proposal, The Composer created the brand based on the prompt and were able to create a unique and above the brand system/identity for the client. After completing the first draft of the design, the client found that the overall identity was fun, but not quite witty, so they added the handmade collage graphics featuring hand gestures. It is in line with the application of baking cookies as hands play an important role complimenting the skills to bake good cookies. The client agreed, and thought is was a cool thing to apply to the packaging and identity.

Client: Baked Global Sdn. Bhd. | Design Agency: The Composer | Creative Direction: Lim Oon Soon-Studio MMCMM | Design: Shawn Chow Hung Yun

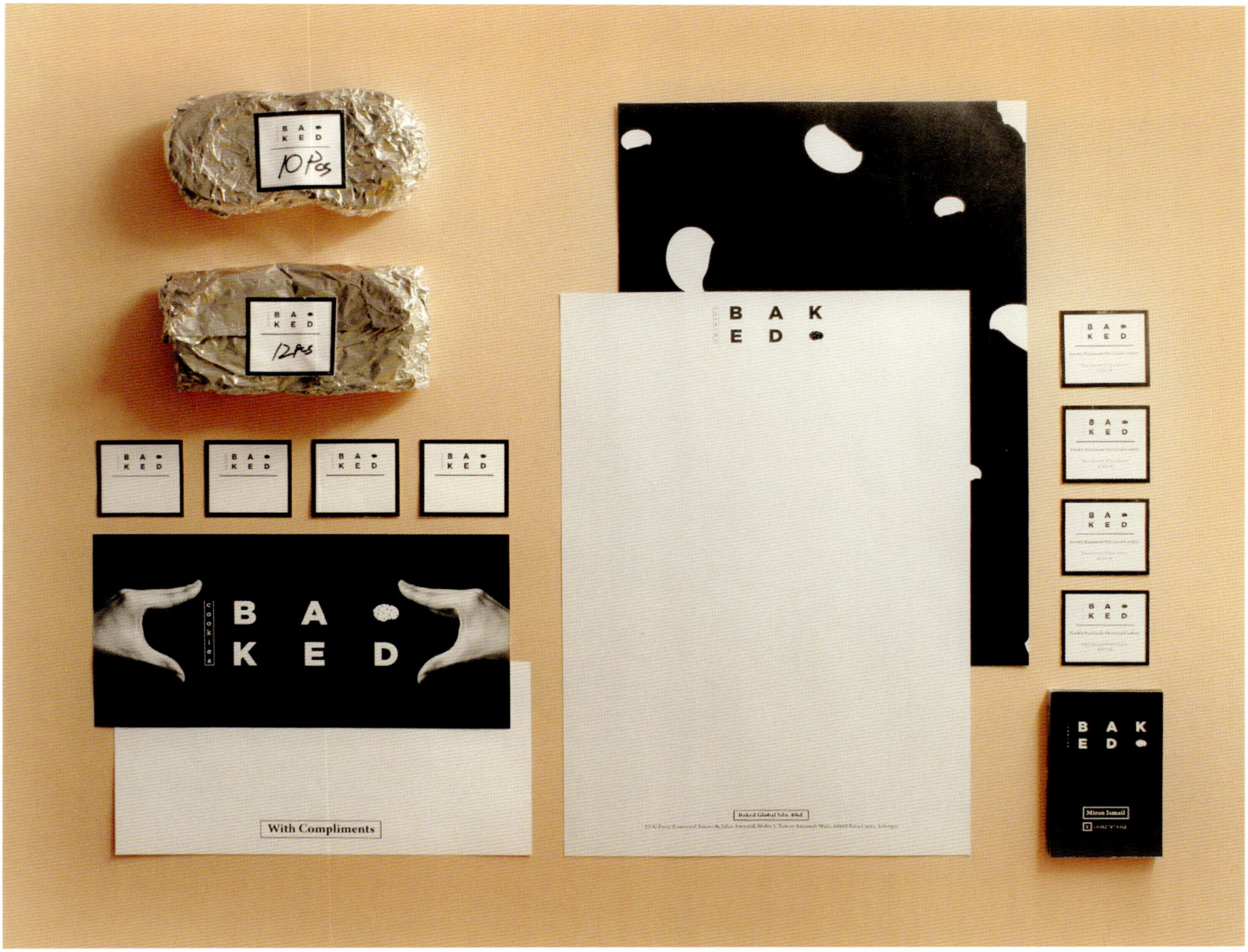

BAKED

10 Pcs

12 Pcs

With Compliments

Baked Global Sdn. Bhd.

Miron Ismail

Leading Search Partners

Leading Search Partners is made up of pearl divers, treasure hunters, and gold-diggers. When it comes to the treasure seekers, a lot search, a few find, but hardly anyone connects. Leading Search Partners sets its aim at successfully mastering all three disciplines. For them, not a single pearl lies too deep, no gold too hidden, and no treasure is too buried.

Client: Leading Search Partners | Design Agency: moodley brand identity | Creative Direction: Mike Fuisz | Art Direction: Nicole Lugitsch | Design: Nicole Lugitsch | Illustration: Malgorzata Bieroza | Photography: Marion Luttenberger | Project Management: Christina Schachner | Web Development: Sissi Bieber

WER WIR SIND LEISTUNGEN KARRIERE-PORTAL NEWS WO WIR SIND

› Executive Search Professional Search Management Audit Branchenkompetenz

Professional Search.

Gründliche Goldgräber durchsuchen jeden Quadratzentimeter ihres Feldes. Wir tun das mit klug ausgearbeiteten, auf das Ziel ausgerichteten Suchstrategien. Ein profundes Vorgehen, um auf unvermutete Kandidaten zu stoßen. Streng nach Plan.

LEISTUNGSBESCHREIBUNG

Wie heißt es so treffend im Englischen? *Leave no stone unturned*, lasse nichts unversucht. Entsprechend motiviert gehen wir beim Professional Search ans Werk. Anhand eines Fünf-Punkte-Plans fördern wir gezielt verborgene Talente zu Tage.

Der erste Punkt: tiefgehend zu analysieren, wo exakt die Erwartungen

eigenen Marktwissen die optimale Suchstrategie zu entwickeln. In Punkt zwei durchforsten wir unsere Datenbanken und Netzwerke, ergänzt mit lockenden Inseraten in ausgewählten Medien.

Als nächstes selektieren wir die Bewerbungen und reden in der Folge persönlich mit den vielversprechendsten Bewerbern. Der Kunde erhält

eine *Shortlist* der verbliebenen Kandidaten. Im vierten Punkt bringen wir Bewerber und Kunden zusammen. Gerne bringen wir unsere Erfahrung auf Wunsch bei diesen Gesprächen ein. Wie wir auch fünftens gerne bei Bedarf bei abschließenden Vertragsverhandlungen fundierte Unterstützung leisten.

Calaveza

Calaveza is a special beer that derives its name from the mixture of the Spanish terms "pumpkin"(calabaza) and "beer" (cerveza). For the packaging, serial illustrations were developed as if they formed part of a family portrait, with one particularity, the heads had been replaced by pumpkins. This resulted in a visual game that links the identity of the beer with its principal ingredient.

Client: Deli_rant | Design Agency: estudio mllongo | Creative Direction: Marisa Llongo

Strangelove

To create a unique looking organic energy drink for the Australian market, the branding needed to specifically speak to the young urban consumer. Strangelove is based loosely around the stories of the creators, who in their youth would burn the candle at both ends. With the overall idea of "repent," an illustrator was commissioned to bring the packaging to life through relevant stories. The unique style of Randy Mora was used as it reflects the idea of craft, quality, and narrative. The front of the packaging deliberately places an illustration on the front to create disruption, and cut-through in a crowded energy drink market where all competition plays a similar game.

Client: Strangelove | Design Agency: The Creative Method | Creative Direction: Tony Ibbotson | Design: Tony Ibbotson, Tim Heyer, Andri Mondong | Illustration: Randy Mora

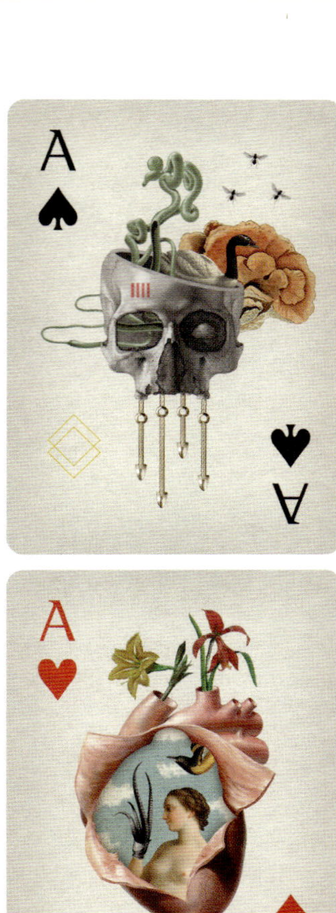
A

K

Q

J

A

K

Q

J

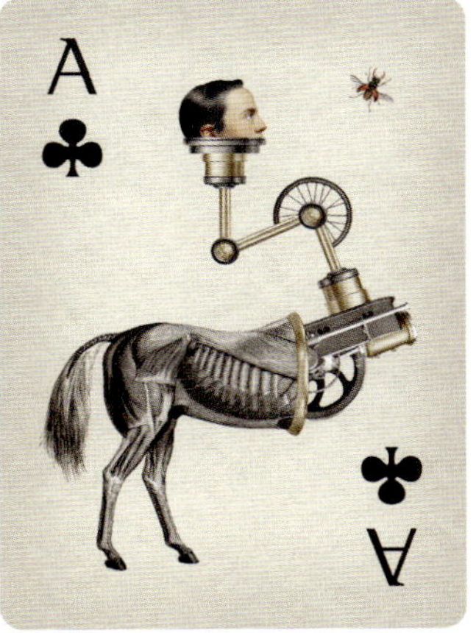
A

K

Q

J

A

K

Q

J

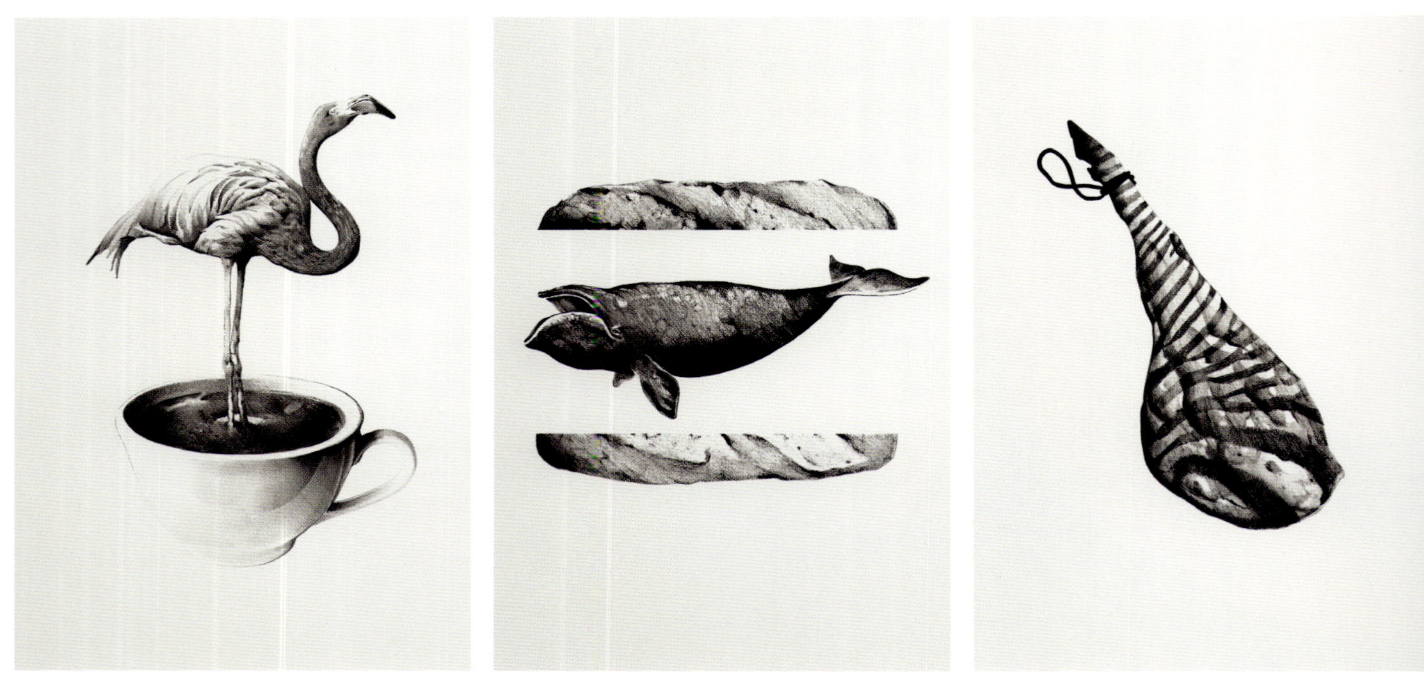

Deli_rant Delicatessen & Restaurant

A former old commercial space located in the historic heart of Valencia has been transformed by studio mllongo into a restaurant and delicatessen shop in a pure New York SoHo style. For this purpose a consonant brand identity was needed, the idea was to create an inseparable whole between both branding and interior design. The primary identity element is not only a logo, but also a symbolic universe with a life of its own.

Client: Deli_rant | Design Agency: estudio mllongo | Design: Marisa Llongo

deli_rant.
delicatessen&restaurant
creu nova, 4
46002 valencia
96 325 89 19
deli-rant@deli-rant.com
deli-rant.com

Fika

Fika Bar & Kitchen, based in Brick Lane, East London, has built a loyal following since its launch in 2008. Fika is named after the Swedish word for coffee break, and Designers Anonymous needed no encouragement to express its "Take a Break" proposition in a way that matches the brand's quirky personality and cosmopolitan location. Their branding solution is based on the notion of a break from the dull routine of daily life. This is subtly expressed by perforating sections around and within a mix of photographs and illustrations. Sections are perforated and removed, and either assembled as collage, or used individually to express a variety of messages. The perforated edging detail links each image back to Fika and the theme of "Take a Break." Altogether, the Fika branding is a feat of joined-up, broken-up thinking.

Client: Fika Bar & Kitchen | Design Agency: Designers Anonymous

LOYALTY REWARD:
GET YOUR 6TH HOT DRINK FREE!

FIKA
BAR & KITCHEN
To Go

Rice Enoir

A packaging submission for Rice Enoir Sake Competition. The design and illustration was created to promote the Japanese town "Setouchi," derived from Seto Inland Sea, which is popular for the fishery business. The illustration depicting a surreal image of a fish man brewing sake was drawn by Roby Dwi Antono.

Client: Rice Enoir | Design Agency: Sciencewerk | Design: Danis Sie | Illustration: Roby Dwi Antono | Photography: Evelina K

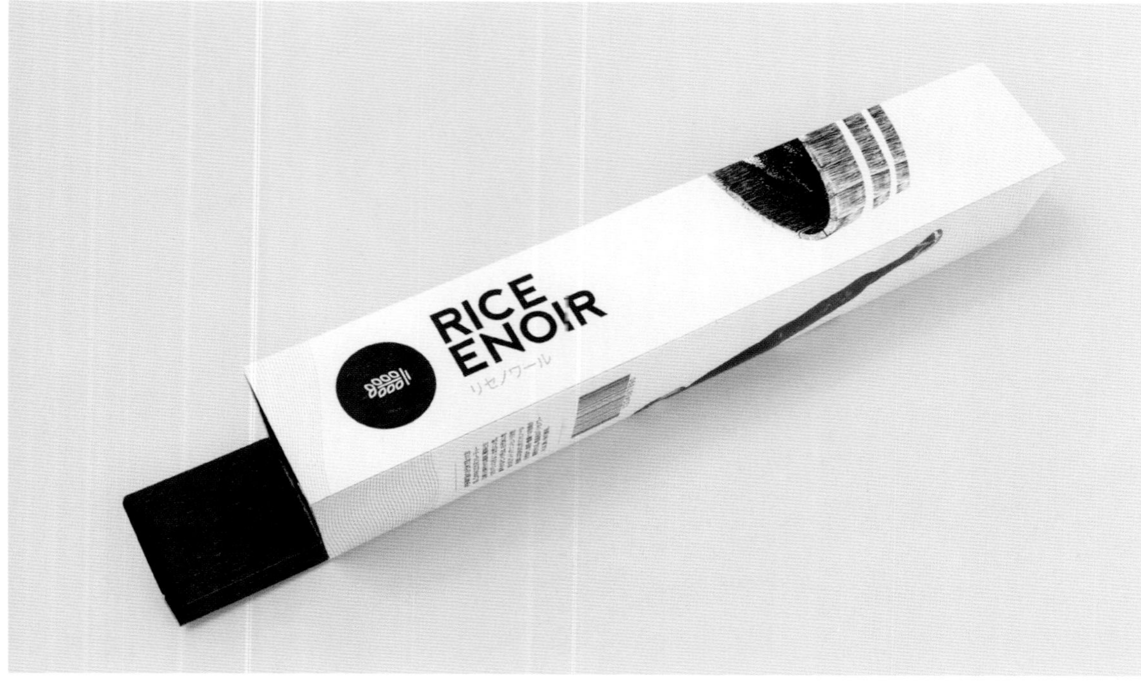

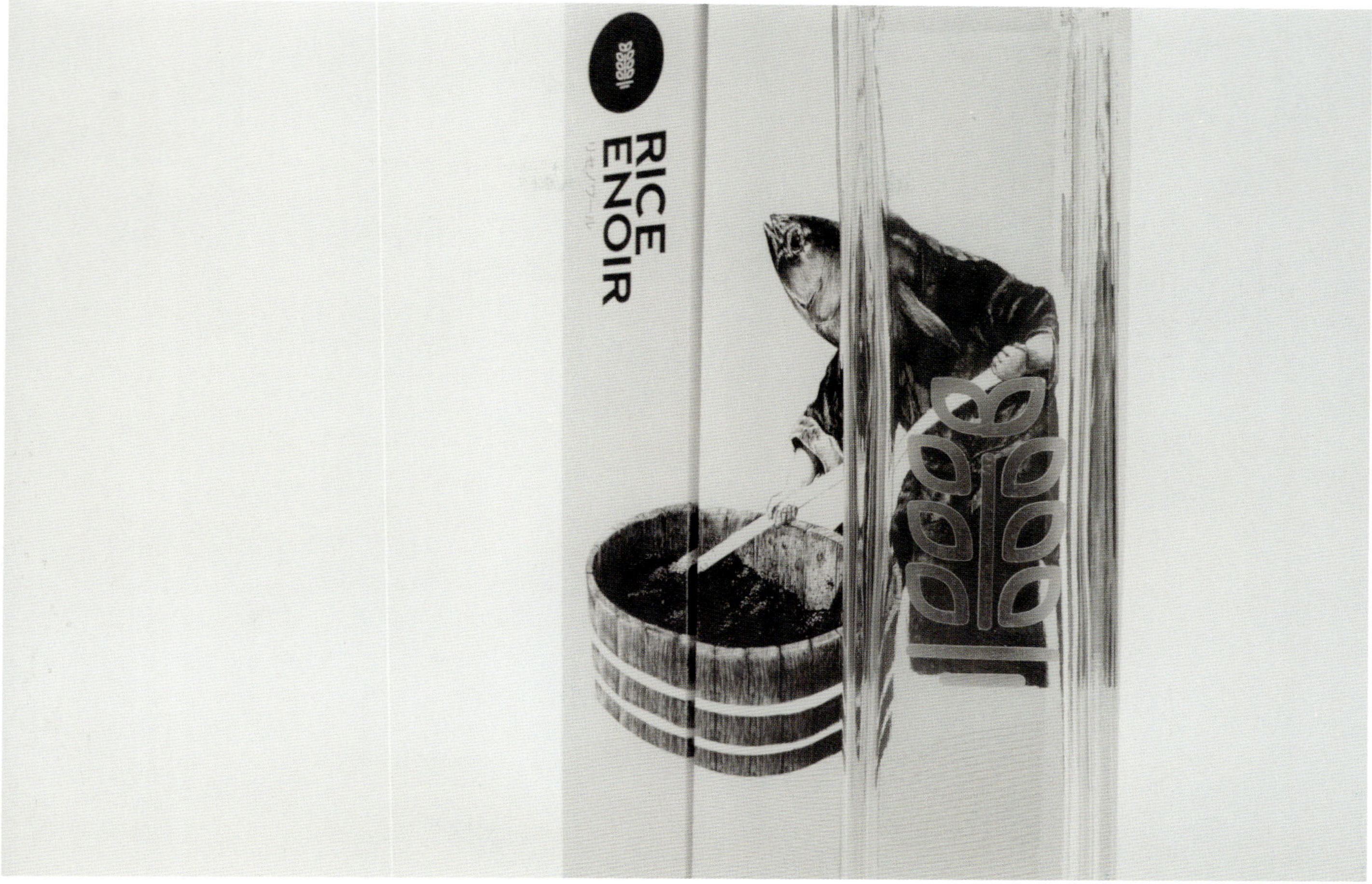
RICE
ENOIR

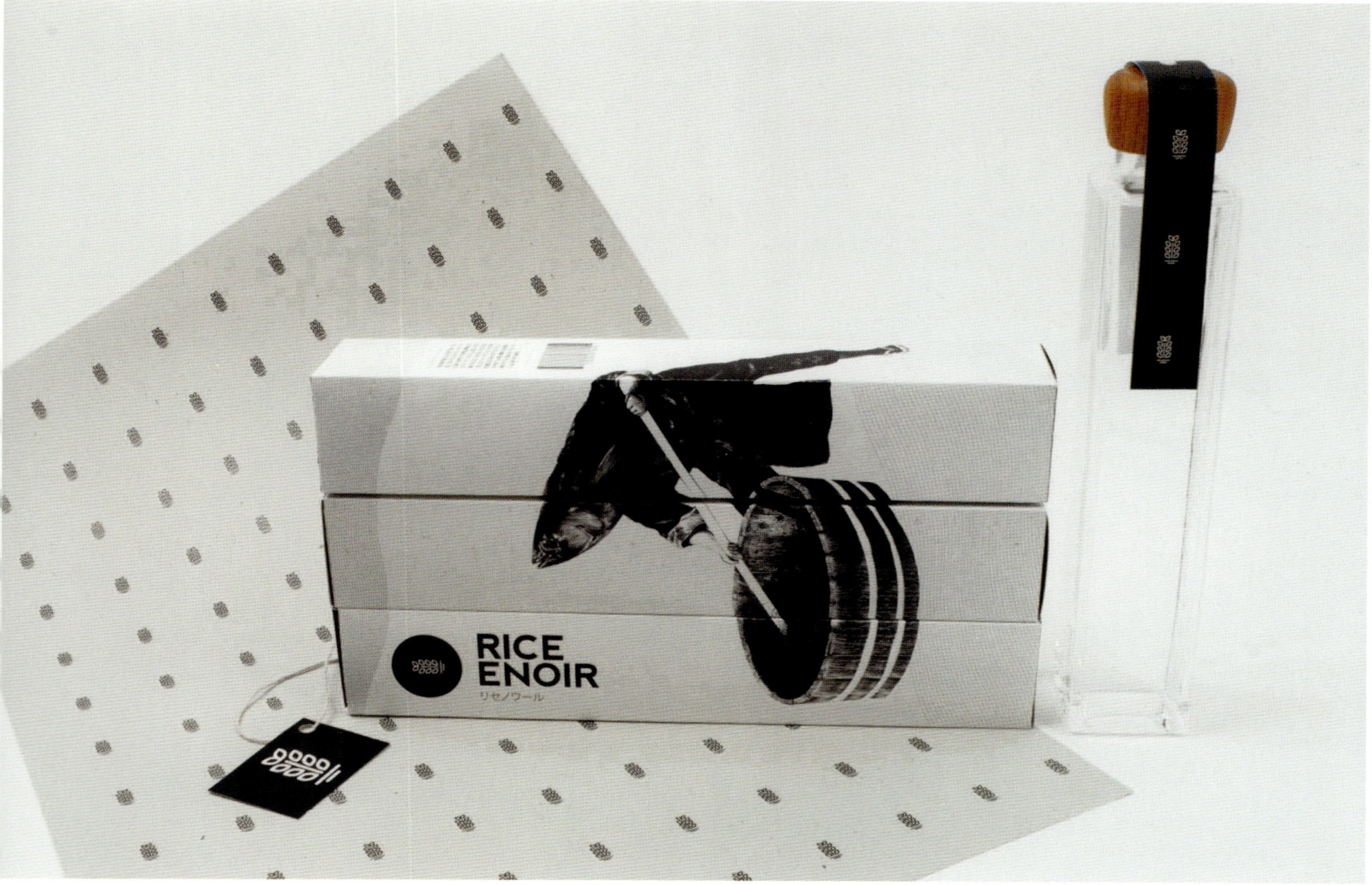
RICE
ENOIR
リセノワール

Absolution

Launched in 2010, Absolution is Isabelle Carron's cosmetics revolution. Certified organic, unisex, and made in France, Absolution is renowned for the quality of its skincare formulas as well as its tremendous global branding. Jak (for Just a Kiss) is a Parisian branding and advertising agency that was created in 2007 by Arnaud Pigounides.

As designer associate on Absolution, he won many awards including the Wallpaper Design Award 2010.

Client: Absolution | Design Agency: Just a Kiss | Design: Arnaud Pigounides

L'Eau Soir et Matin
absolution
La Solution + ENERGIE
absolution
La Solution + ANTI-AGE
absolution
La Crème du Jour
absolution
absolution
La Solution + CONTROLE
absolution
La Crème de l'Homme
absolution
absolution

Sh‘g’oes

Design Studio of Both came up with the final touches for a clean and elegant new brand identity for a high-quality women's shoe boutique.

Client: Sh‘g’oes | Design Agency: Design Studio of Both | Creative Direction: Àxel Durana | Illustration: Various Autors

Filirea Gi Wine

Packaging design for limited production homemade wine. The illustration depicts the process of creating wine from the harvest to the bottling. Printed with silk-screen printing method on paper that is wrapped around the bottle to convey the sense of handmade.

Client: Zafeiriadis Paschalis | Design: Zafeiriadis Christos

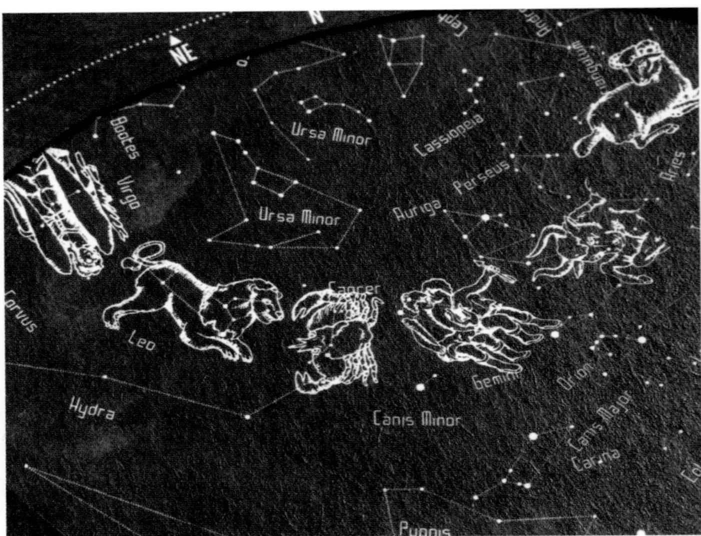

Space Explore

This is a teaching kit for a space club. Through this teaching kit, the audience learns more about outer space and constellations, such as how to find stars using a star map, and stargazing. The concept of the teaching kit is, 'camping in space.' The kit encourages people to 'camp' in outer space, to get together with friends, and explore unknown knowledge in space.

Client: Space Club | Design Agency: Fundamental

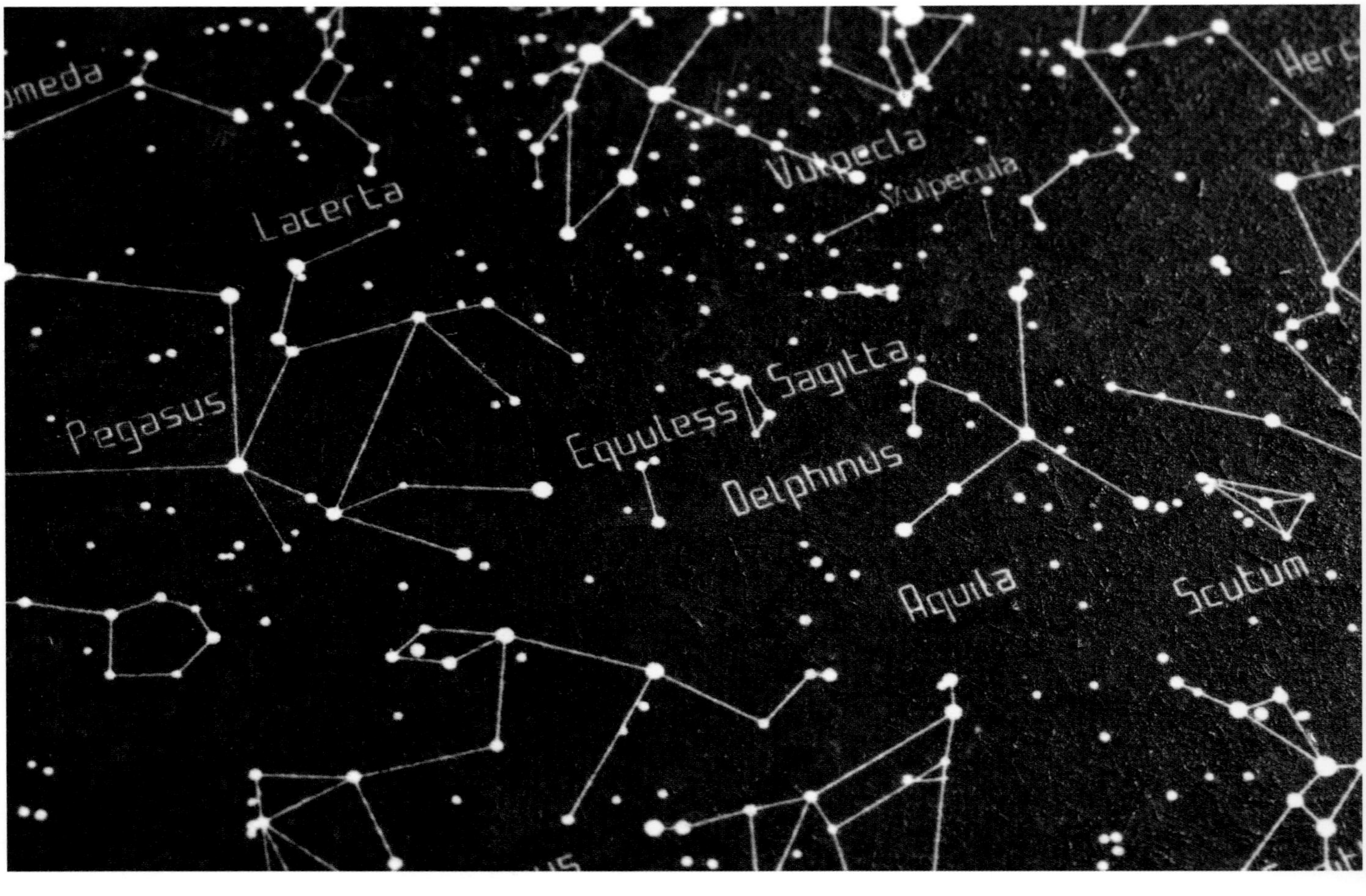

The Space explore
everyone can be the space explorer
Teaching kit
The Space explore
The Space explore
everyone can be the space explorer
The Space explore
Game Cards

Stage01
Getting Start
A pair of bright eyes, a small flashlight covered with red cellophane and a star map are all you need. Binoculars is a plus but not a must. You don't need telescope unless you want to study the deep sky objects like nebulae and clusters or the planetary features. But then you won't be able to spot a whole constellation as the eld of vision is too narrow.
Don't forget to bring along a jacket with you as the temperature will fall at night.
A flashlight
A pair of bright eyes
A Binoculars
A star map

208 Duecento Otto

208 Duecento Otto is a restaurant that gets its name from its location on Hollywood Road 208. This two-story restaurant is filled with a strong atmosphere of art and design. The bottom floor is a lively bar while the upper floor is a tranquil restaurant. Both floors offer al fresco dining with great view of Hollywood Road.

The logo design was based on the restaurant's address 208 and the outline of its door plate, which simply and clearly featured the location of the restaurant. it's visual image was based on the concept of Mind Map, connecting the many shapes and patterns formed by the people and food in the restaurant. In a relaxed artistic mood, its shows all the possibilities and relationships between the people, food and the restaurant, thereby creating an unforgettable uniqueness for the brand.

Client: 208 Duecento Otto | Design Agency: c plus c workshop

208
DUECENTO OTTO
www.208.com.hk
ABOUT PIZZA NAPOLETANA

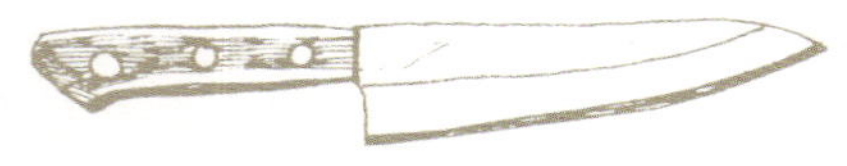

Festival del Baccalà 2012

Festival del Baccalà is a traveling contest between local restaurants of Northern Italy. The restaurants challenge each other by proposing their own interpretation of the Baccalà's tradition. Dry Design's goal was to project an elegant but fresh communication, so they chose this combination of strong typography and nostalgic illustrations. They then thought about an original way to display the brochures, and decided to display them inside a metal can typically used for fish fillet's storage. They customized the cans for the occasion, and placed them on the counter with the brochures inside.

Client: Tagliapietra srl | Design Agency: Dry Design | Design: Carolina Cloos, Francesca Mezzetti | Photography: Francesca Mezzetti

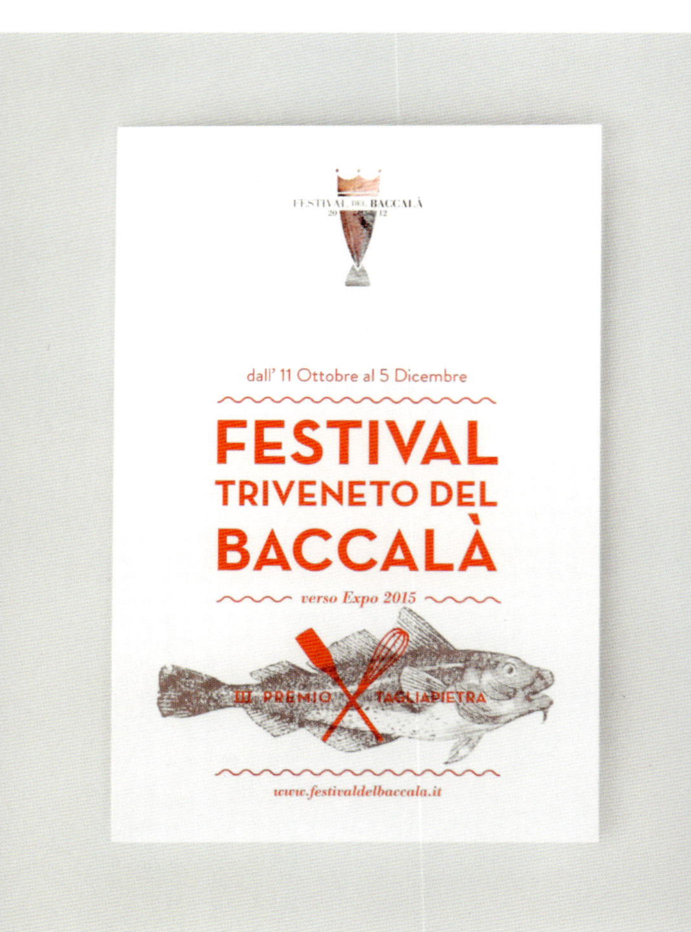
FESTIVAL DEL BACCALÀ
2012
dall' 11 Ottobre al 5 Dicembre
FESTIVAL
TRIVENETO DEL
BACCALÀ
verso Expo 2015
III PREMIO
TAGLIAPIETRA
www.festivaldelbaccala.it

dall' 11 Ottobre al 5 Dicembre
FESTIVAL
TRIVENETO DEL
BACCALÀ
verso Expo 2015
III PREMIO
TAGLIAPIETRA
www.festivaldelbaccala.it

Servus am Marktplatz

"Servus am Marktplatz" is an online store full of handmade goods that were produced with care and skill – and customers can feel it: not only while browsing through the webshop, but especially when they unwrap their parcel. Every single one is packed individually using tissue paper, cloth, and cardboard instead of bubble wrap and plastic. High quality packaging for high quality products. moodley designed the whole Servus shop experience from UI/UX to the packaging concept.

Client: Red Bull Media House | Design Agency: moodley brand identity | Creative Direction: Mike Fuisz | Art Direction: Sabine Kernbichler, Nicole Lugitsch | Design: Sabine Kernbichler, Nicole Lugitsch | Illustration: Reinhard Blumenschein (Weinper&Co GmbH, Wien) | Photography: Tina Reiter | Brand Consulting: Caro Frank (Caro Frank Markenberatung) | Text: Rita Stahlberg, Sarah Posch | Project Management moodley: Markus Supanitsch

Servus
Gutes von Daheim.
Mit LIEBE
Ein Gruß aus der Heimat
Ein Stückchen Heimat

Angekommen.

Matías Fiori Personal Card

Matías Fiori is a young and fresh graphic designer from Uruguay with clients all around the world, including Barcelona, England, Brazil, and many other countries. He is the co-founder of re-robot studio, based in Montevideo, Uruguay. He needed affordable and simple personal cards for his self promotion that not only showed his infomation, but also his essence as a person and as a Designer (or at least part of it).

Design: Matías Fiori

PAPA-RA-PA-PA-PA!
CHIRLO
CHIRLO
LUMINOSA
pica!
¡fuck off!
¡fuck off!
PAPA-RA-PA-PA-PA!
CULITO
PAPA-RA-PA-PA-PA!
¡fuck off!

WILD COMBO
FUMMER & FISKARS
CO-OP
KUUN 3. LAUANTAI
SILTASESSA
DISCO / HOUSE / ROCK

WILD COMBO
FUMMER & FISKARS
CO-OP
KUUN 3. LAUANTAI
SILTASESSA
DISCO / HOUSE / ROCK
WELL
DONE TO
THE IDIOT
WHO RAN
OVER MY
PET LIZZARD

WILD COMBO
FUMMER & FISKARS
CO-OP
KUUN 3. LAUANTAI
SILTASESSA
DISCO / HOUSE / ROCK

WILD COMBO
FUMMER & FISKARS
CO-OP
KUUN 3. LAUANTAI
SILTASESSA
DISCO / HOUSE / ROCK

WILD COMBO
FUMMER & FISKARS
CO-OP
KUUN 3. LAUANTAI
SILTASESSA
DISCO / HOUSE / ROCK
THAT'S
REAL
FUCKIN'
NEATO

WILD COMBO
FUMMER & FISKARS
CO-OP
KUUN 3. LAUANTAI
SILTASESSA
DISCO / HOUSE / ROCK
FF

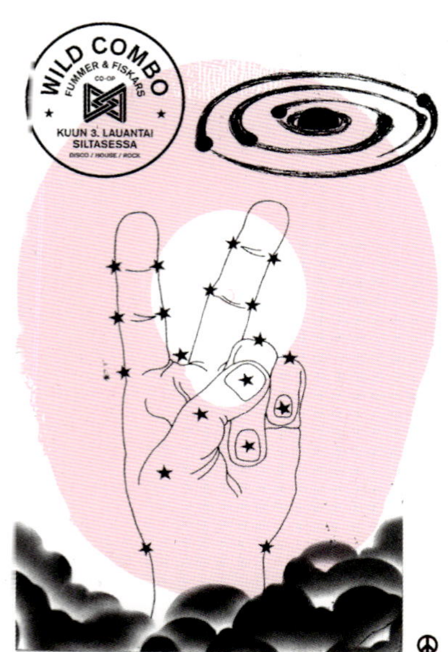
WILD COMBO
FUMMER & FISKARS
CO-OP
KUUN 3. LAUANTAI
SILTASESSA
DISCO / HOUSE / ROCK

WILD COMBO
FUMMER & FISKARS
CO-OP
KUUN 3. LAUANTAI
SILTASESSA
DISCO / HOUSE / ROCK

Wild Combo

Identity for Wild Combo, arguably the best club in Helsinki. Their aim is to surprise positively and avoid tinkering.

Client: Siltanen | Design: Leo Karhunen

Scent Library

Scent Library believes that scents have the extraordinary power to send us back in time, and bring memories to life. It thus sets out to curate scent products from all over the world, in hope that each person will find that perfect scent to match a memory. As a non-conventional library filled with scents, a unique librarian is required. Mr. Hummingbird was therefore created to fulfill this role. Whilst busying himself handpicking scents from around the world, Mr. Hummingbird is also responsible for recommending scents based on his vast knowledge about the field.

Client: Scent Library | Design Agency: The Folks Studio | Design: Yeo Zhengliang, Soon Siew Hui | Copywriter: Soon Siew Hui | Illustration: Yeo Zhengliang | Photography: Yeo Zhengliang, Soon Siew Hui

SCENT
LIBRARY
"The search for great scents never ends."
Mr Hummingbird
www.scentlibrary.asia
Jodie
@scentlibrary.asia
facebook.com/scentlibrary
www.scentlibrary.asia

MR HUMMINGBIRD'S NOTE
Hope you like it !
BRAND:
Glasshouse Fragrances
TYPE:
Candle
ORIGIN:
Australia
DESCRIPTION:
Exotic blend of water lily, spring orange blossom, precious woods and amber. Refreshes like a monsoon rain.
"The search for great scents never ends."
Mr Hummingbird

Pronto

In this project, Daria Karpenko created new branding for Pronto, a chain of Italian restaurants. Her solution was to change the visual aesthetic from one that was mostly bright pink, which could repulse target audiences, to one reflecting classical Italian motifs. The word "Pronto" has a couple meanings: "quick" in English and "ready" in Italian. The new logo works with both of these meanings: the winged hat references the Roman God Mercury, famous for his high speed, while the chef hat defines it as a restaurant.

Client: Pronto | Design: Daria Karpenko | Photography: Anton Demidov

PRONTO
delivery
PRONTO
delivery

PRONTO
cafe italiano
Dear Ms. Jones.
I am seeking a position in your engineering department where I may use my training in computer sciences to solve Taylor's engineering problems. I would like to be a part of the department that developed the Internet Selection System but am unsure whether you have a current opening.
I expect to receive a Bachelor of Science degree in Engineering from North Carolina State University in June and by that time will have completed the Computer Systems Engineering Program. Since September 2000, I have been participating, through the University, in the Professional Training Program at Computer Systems International in Raleigh. In the program I was assigned to several staff sections as an apprentice. Most recently, I have been a programmer trainee in the Engineering Department and have gained a great deal of experience in computer applications. Details of the academic courses I have taken are included in the enclosed resume.
If there is a position open at Taylor Inc., please let me know whom I should contact for further information. I look forward to hearing from you soon. I may be reached at my office (919-866-4000 ext. 232) or via email (Brock@pronto.ru).
Sincerely,
Rebecca Brock
PRONTO
delivery
PRONTO
cafe italiano
PRONTO
cafe italiano
Moscow, Solyanka street, 6/2
8 (495) 616-72-11

Lupains

21 recipes for grain bread, destined for craftsmen bakers, could not be more of a beautiful inspiration. The mill company of Bachasson asked Les Bons Faiseurs to design the new visual identity for the brand Lupains. The grains displayed, as if in a herbarium, illustrate each recipe in a very precise and poetic way, creating a strong, and at the same time, clear visual identity.

Client: Moulins de Bachasson | Design Agency: Les Bons Faiseurs | Creative Direction: Etienne Rothe | Art Direction: Fanny Katz

LUPAINS
DES GRAINES, DES MAINS, DES PAINS

LUPAINS
MAXI FIBRES

LUPAINS
TOURNESOL

LUPAINS
TROIS GRAINES

LUPAINS
MAXI FIBRES

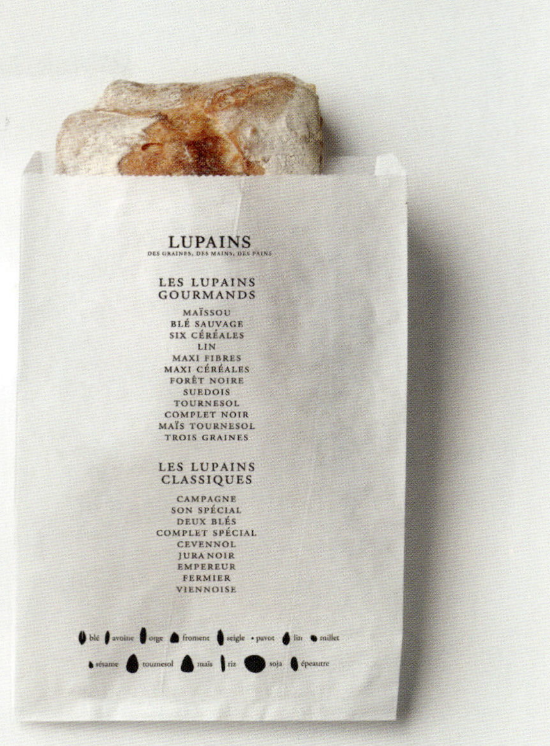
LUPAINS
DES GRAINES, DES MAINS, DES PAINS
LES LUPAINS GOURMANDS
MAÏSSOU
BLÉ SAUVAGE
SIX CÉRÉALES
LIN
MAXI FIBRES
MAXI CÉRÉALES
FORÊT NOIRE
SUEDOIS
TOURNESOL
COMPLET NOIR
MAÏS TOURNESOL
TROIS GRAINES
LES LUPAINS CLASSIQUES
CAMPAGNE
SON SPÉCIAL
DEUX BLÉS
COMPLET SPÉCIAL
CEVENNOL
JURA NOIR
EMPEREUR
FERMIER
VIENNOISE
blé avoine orge froment seigle pavot lin millet
sésame tournesol maïs riz soja épeautre

LUPAINS
DES GRAINES, DES MAINS, DES PAINS
LUPAINS
TOURNESOL
LUPAINS
TROIS GRAINES

Sugarillos

This work is mousegraphics's very conscious decision to visually transcribe the client's first and second wish – "can we show people that, this lot of sugar is actually a spoonful of sugar? Can we also make a nice sugar pack that people will buy to decorate their table or cup with?" To be both, the packaging had to be very matter-of-fact about the content (quantity), and quite straightforward as to this content's value (quality) and special aesthetics (packaging).

The result is as sincere as a design can possibly get, without the connotations of "boring."

Client: Sugarillos | Design Agency: mousegraphics

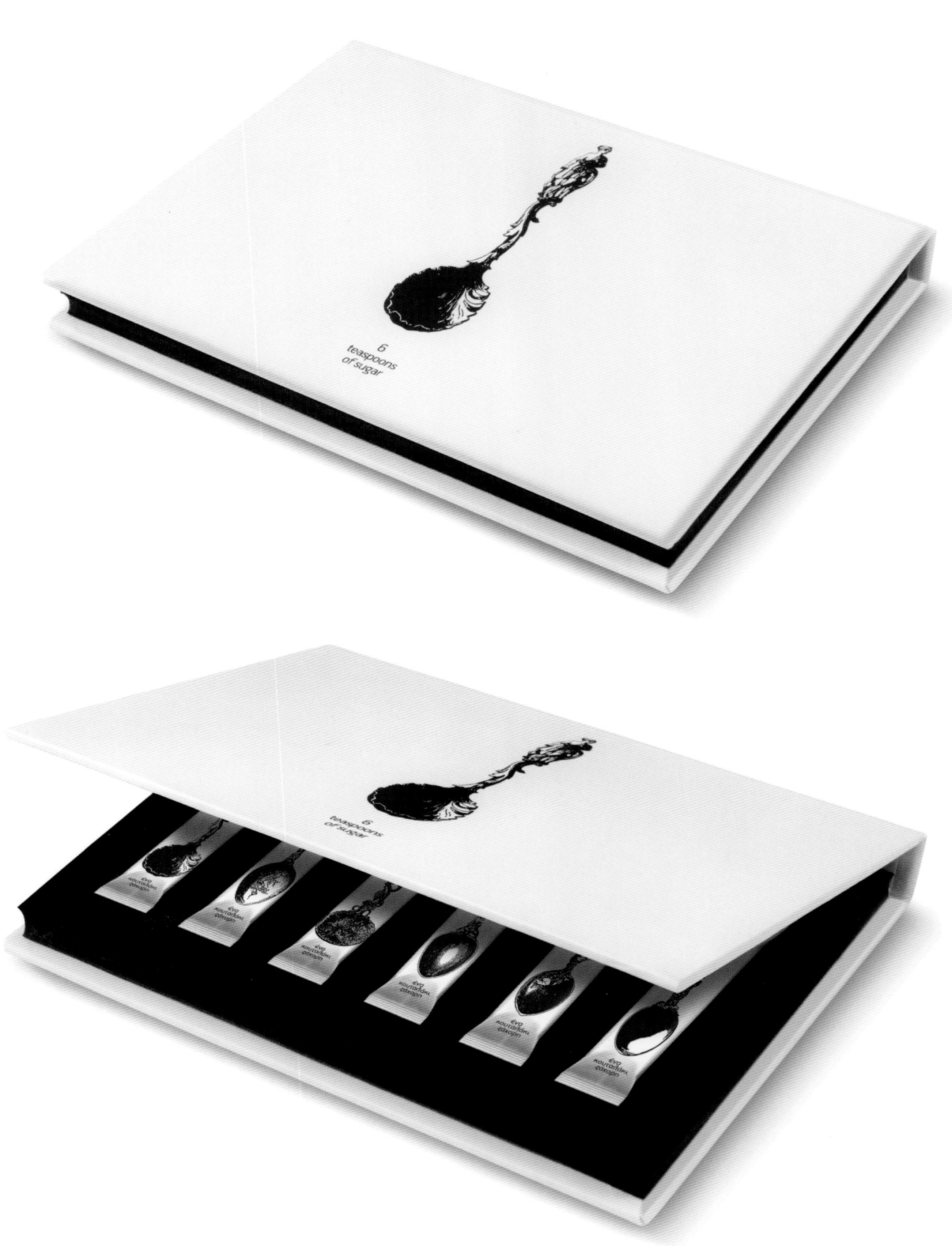
6
teaspoons
of sugar

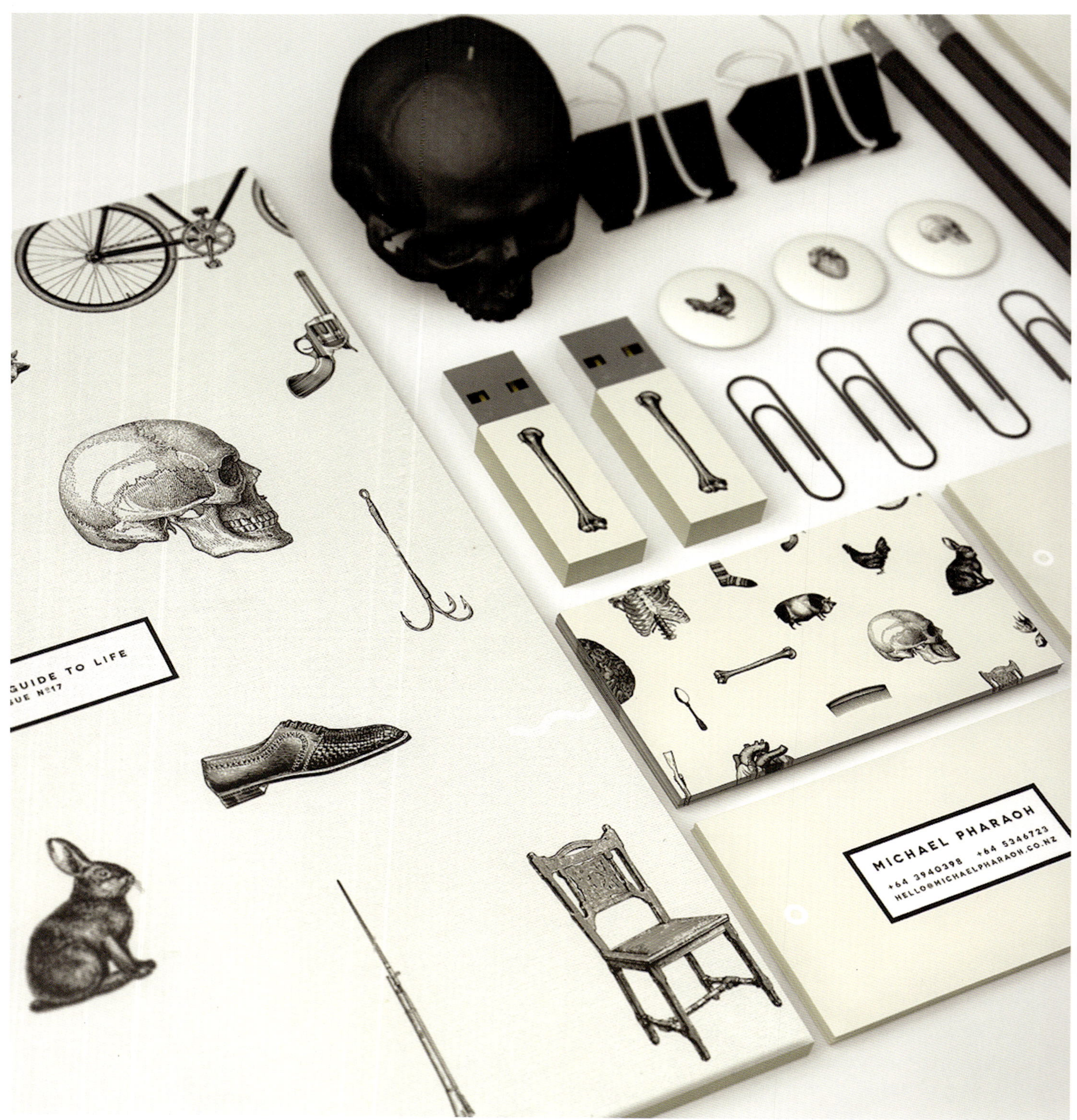

Michaels Guide to Life

"Michaels Guide to Life" was a personal project where Michael Pharaoh wanted to create a go-to guidebook for life. The book contains what he thinks are the most important things he has learned in his life so far, as well as things he thinks everyone should probably know. The heart of this branding revolves around the Victorian style of illustration he used. You will see it throughout the book, and also in most of the collateral. It was also important to Michael for this book to look simple and approachable.

Client: Michaels Guide to Life (Personal) | Design: Michael Pharaoh

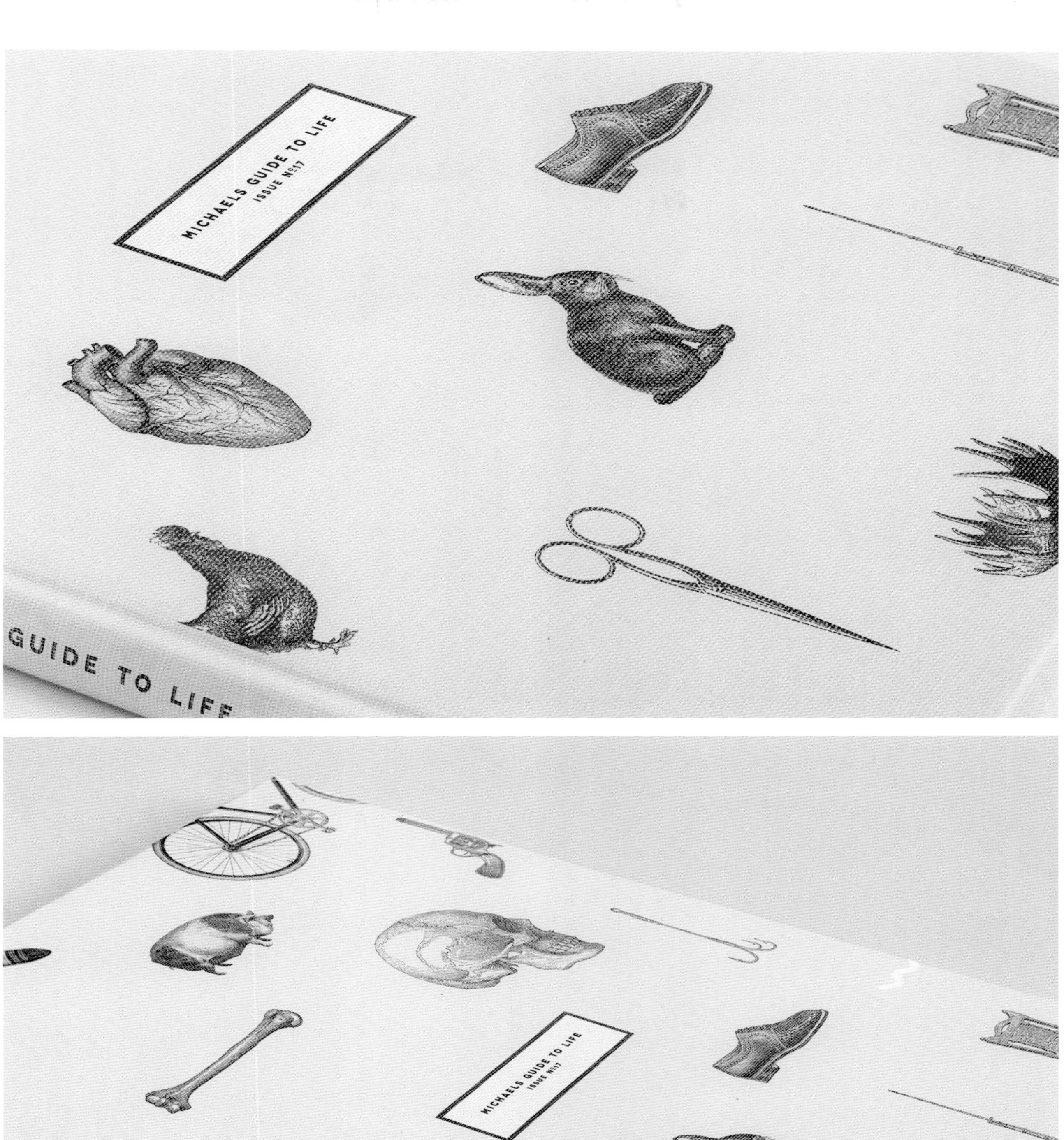
MICHAELS GUIDE TO LIFE
ISSUE No17
GUIDE TO LIFE
MICHAELS GUIDE TO LIFE
ISSUE No17
MICHAELS GUIDE TO LIFE

Urban Seed

Urban Seed is a non-profit organization that exists to inspire a new generation of people to build relationships with healthy food, farming, and the land. Through educational development programs, Urban Seed provides an outlet for community enrichment while supplying fresh, local produce. The organization is located on Dudley Farm in Nashville, Tennessee.

The 5th annual Field-to-Fork benefit dinner serves to promote the ideals of Urban Seed. The purpose of the dinner is to raise awareness and funding for the organization while giving participants a genuine dining experience. The event is located on the farm itself, bringing people directly to the source of their food. Participants should leave with a better understanding of Urban Seed, and feel motivated to support the organization financially. Deliverables for the farm, organization, and benefit dinner all needed to perform in a cohesive manner. Inspired by a utilitarian mindset, black ink was chosen to aid in this cohesion while being budget conscious. The monochromatic paper selection also created harmony for the project.

Client: Urban Seed | Designer: Caroline Morris

Kohlrabi
BEET
White
ONIONS
Broad Leaved
ENDIVE

Field-to-Fork
DINNER MENU
FARM PRODUCTS HARVESTED JUST A FEW FEET AWAY
FARMSTEAD DUCK HAM & PEAR SALAD
ANSON MILLS GRITS
GUINEA & DUMPLINGS
SEARED NORTH CAROLINA MOUNTAIN TROUT
GRILLED BORDER SPRINGS LAMB
DUDLEY FARM FROMAGE BLANC
CHOCOLATELLA
URBAN SEED

405
LIBRARY
BIBLIOTECA

BUENOS
DAYS!
YOUR
MUNDO
AQUÍ & AWAY
CITY MAESTRO
MERCI
take it despacio
BUEN VOYAGE
For you
HOLA
FRIEND!
VIVALALIFE
NW
W
N
SW
NE
S
E
SE

MODERNISMO
QUADRAT D'OR

A SURREAL WORLD

MUCHO
ARTE

"I AM NOT STRANGE,
I'M JUST NOT NORMAL"
Salvador Dalí

MIRÓ
DALÍ
SERRAT
PERET
J. VERDAGUER
C. RUIZ ZAFÓN
TÀPIES
JOSEP PLA
LA PLAZA
DEL DIAMANTE
de Mercè Rodoreda

HEEL Athens Lab

More than a clothing brand, Heel proposes an alternative production model. The new corporate design aims to create the unique world of Heel, where the corporate values of optimism, team work, ecology, and modern urban lifestyle are highlighted.

The "look & feel" elements of the new identity combine illustrations inspired by nature and city life, along with messages that express everyday life emotions, framed by a unique triangle pattern.

Last but not least, a very important element of the new identity is the Heel Font, which was especially designed for the company in order to emphasize the spontaneous and ingenuous aspects of the brand culture and philosophy.

Client: HEEL Athens Lab | Design Agency: Pi6 Communication Design

HEEL
ATHENS LAB
I LOVE ATHENS!
WWW.HEELSHOP.GR
ΒΛΕΠΩ ΣΤΕΡΙΑ!
WWW.HEELSHOP.GR
ΤΙ ΒΛΕΠΟΥΝ ΤΑ ΜΑΤΑΚΙΑ ΜΟΥ
WWW.HEELSHOP.GR
ΠΑΜΕ ΠΟΔΗΛΑΤΑΔΑ ΜΕΧΡΙ ΤΗ ΘΑΛΑΣΣΑ?
WWW.HEELSHOP.GR
HELLO! IS ANYBODY THERE?
WWW.HEELSHOP.GR
ΛΑΤΡΕΥΩ ΤΟΝ ΚΑΘΑΡΟ ΟΥΡΑΝΟ
WWW.HEELSHOP.GR
ΚΛΕΙΣΤΕ ΤΑ ΦΩΤΑ
WWW.HEELSHOP.GR
ΩΡΑΙΑ ΘΕΑ
WWW.HEELSHOP.GR
ΜΥΡΙΖΩ ΥΠΕΡΟΧΑ
WWW.HEELSHOP.GR
ΓΙΝΟΜΑΣΤΕ Η ΑΛΛΑΓΗ ΤΟΥ ΚΟΣΜΟΥ ΠΟΥ ΘΕΛΟΥΜΕ ΝΑ ΔΟΥΜΕ!
ΚΑΤΙ ΠΕΡΙΣΣΟΤΕΡΟ ΑΠΟ ΜΙΑ ΕΤΑΙΡΕΙΑ ΕΝΔΥΜΑΤΩΝ, Η HEEL ΠΡΟΤΕΙΝΕΙ ΕΝΑ ΕΝΑΛΛΑΚΤΙΚΟ ΜΟΝΤΕΛΟ ΠΑΡΑΓΩΓΗΣ, ΠΟΥ ΒΑΣΙΖΕΤΑΙ ΣΤΗΝ ΟΜΑΔΙΚΟΤΗΤΑ, ΣΤΗΝ ΙΣΟΤΗΤΑ ΚΑΙ ΣΤΗΝ ΕΡΓΑΣΙΑ ΜΕ ΔΙΚΑΙΟΥΣ ΟΡΟΥΣ. ΜΕΣΑ Σ' ΕΝΑ ΧΩΡΟ ΟΠΟΥ ΟΙ ΠΕΡΙΣΣΟΤΕΡΟΙ ΑΝΑΖΗΤΟΥΝ ΤΟΝ ΕΥΚΟΛΟ ΔΡΟΜΟ, ΕΜΕΙΣ ΤΑΙΡΙΑΖΟΥΜΕ Σ' ΕΝΑΝ ΚΟΣΜΟ ΔΗΜΙΟΥΡΓΙΚΟΤΗΤΑΣ, ΑΝΤΙΣΤΑΣΗΣ ΚΑΙ ΕΛΕΥΘΕΡΙΑΣ. ΣΧΕΔΙΑΖΟΥΜΕ ΚΑΙ ΠΑΡΑΓΟΥΜΕ ΤΑ ΠΡΟΙΟΝΤΑ ΜΑΣ ΣΤΗΝ ΕΛΛΑΔΑ, ΔΙΝΟΝΤΑΣ ΕΜΦΑΣΗ ΣΤΗΝ ΙΔΙΑΙΤΕΡΟΤΗΤΑ ΤΟΥ ΡΟΥΧΟΥ. ΧΡΗΣΙΜΟΠΟΙΟΥΜΕ ΤΗΝ ΜΟΔΑ ΩΣ ΜΕΣΟ ΕΚΦΡΑΣΗΣ ΤΩΝ ΑΝΗΣΥΧΙΩΝ ΜΑΣ ΓΙΑ ΤΗ ΖΩΗ ΚΑΙ ΤΗ ΦΥΣΗ, ΑΠΟ ΤΗΝ ΟΠΟΙΑ ΑΝΤΛΟΥΜΕ ΕΜΠΝΕΥΣΗ ΓΙΑ ΤΟΝ ΣΧΕΔΙΑΣΜΟ ΤΟΥΣ.
WWW.HEELSHOP.GR
Η HEEL ΠΡΟΣΤΑΤΕΥΕΙ ΤΑ ΑΔΕΣΠΟΤΑ ΖΩΑ ΥΠΟΣΤΗΡΙΖΟΝΤΑΣ ΤΗΝ ΟΡΓΑΝΩΣΗ
Η ΑΓΑΠΗ
WWW.HEEL.GR
Η HEEL ΑΓΑΠΑ ΤΗ ΜΕΣΟΓΕΙΟ ΥΠΟΣΤΗΡΙΖΕΙ ΤΟ ΑΡΧΙΠΕΛΑΓΟΣ
Ο ΙΔΑΝΙΚΟΣ ΣΚΥΛΟΣ
HEEL
ATHENS LAB
ΚΑΡΤΑ ΑΛΛΑΓΗΣ
HEEL
ATHENS LAB

HEEL
ATHENS LAB

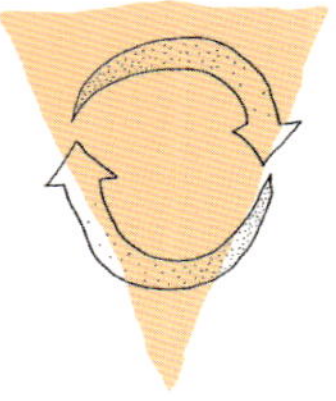

ECO
FRIENDLY

HEEL
ATHENS LAB

100%
COTTON

HEEL
ATHENS LAB

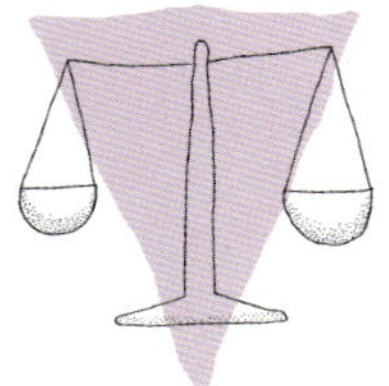

ETHICAL
AWARENESS

HEEL
ATHENS LAB

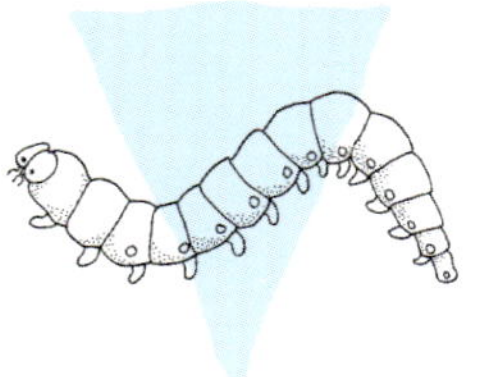

100%
SILK

HEEL
ATHENS LAB

100%
LINEN

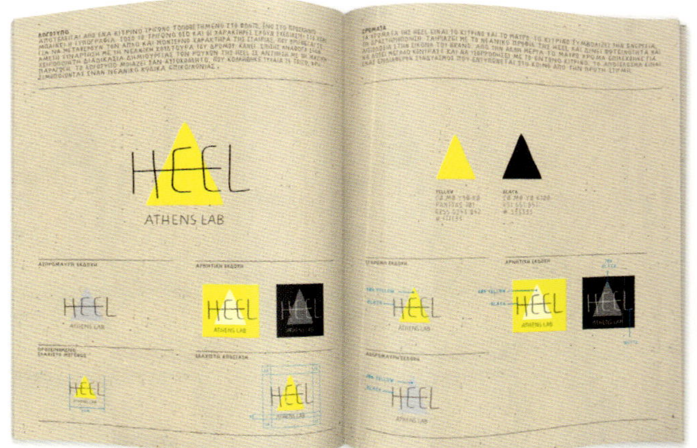

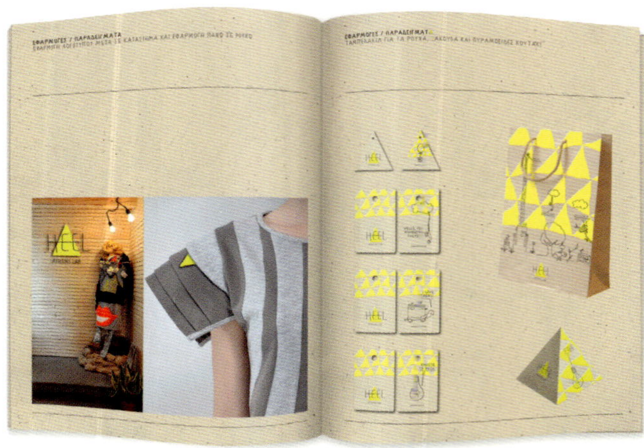

HEEL
ATHENS LAB

ΚΛΕΙΣΤΕ
ΤΑ ΦΩΤΑ
WWW.HEEL.GR
Ο ΙΔΑΝΙΚΟΣ ΣΚΥΛΟΣ

Playlab

Identity and stationery for Playlab, a workshop space aimed to be a creative playground for stressed adults. The Illustrations used are a mixture of scientific elements and random fun images. The stationery is printed in fluorescent Pantone colors, while the actual logo is just blind embossed. The address details are filled in using a rubber stamp.

Client: Playlab | Design Agency: Mind Design | Illustration: Craig Sinnamon

Paul Pethick
Unit 214
The Old Gramophone Works
326 Kensal Road
London W10 5BZ
T: +44 (0)7768 362 575
E: info@playlab.tv
W: www.playlab.tv

Circus

Identity for a new club and restaurant with a burlesque theme and changing performances. Since the club interior features many mirrored surfaces, the design of the logo is based on the shape of a kaleidoscope. The outline shape and basic construction of the logo always remains the same, while the inside changes depending on its application. Other influences came from Surrealism, Art Deco, Alice in Wonderland, animals, and the steps leading up to the large table that doubles as a stage. A main feature of the interior is a 3-dimensional version of the logo built from different layers of perspex, set into a wall, and illuminated from the back in changing colors. Collaboration with Design Research Studio.

Client: Circus | Design Agency: Mind Design | Creative Direction: Holger Jacobs | Art Direction: Craig Sinnamon | Design: Andy Lang, Sara Streule | Interior Design: Tom Dixon, Design Research Studio

SALMON TARTARE 8.95
CKEN WINGS 6.95
ALL OF OUR MEATS ARE COOKED IN A CLASSIC CHARCOAL OVEN.
DESSERTS
VANILLA AND BOURBON RAISIN NEW YORK CHEESECAKE £ 6.00
served with cream or ice cream
PLUM TARTE TATIN 6.00
with cinnamon sugar and vanilla ice cream (15 minutes preparation time)
PEANUT BUTTER AND CHOCOLATE BROWNIE 6.00
with 3 milk ice cream
WARMED APPLE GINGERBREAD 6.00
with light cream cheese mousse and lemon peel syrup

MENU
SMALL
CRISPY FRIED BABY SQUID
RED AND GOLDEN BEET SALAD
GRILLED LANGOUSTINES
BEEF RENDANG EMPANADAS
SCALLOPS IN SHELL
PULLED PORK WITH POTATO LATKES
TUNA AND SALMON TARTARE
SNAPPER CEVICHE
SMOKED STUFFED CHICKEN WINGS
MIXED LEAVES
NEAL'S YARD CHEESE
LARGE
FLATBREAD VEGETABLE PARCELS
SEAFOOD JAMBALAYA OF MARKET SEAFOOD
ADOBO CHICKEN
PAN-FRIED SNAPPER
RED ANGEL HAIR PASTA
CORNBREAD-CRUSTED WIENER SCHNITZEL
24 HOUR SLOW ROASTED BEEF SHORT RIBS
CHURRASCO AND LANGOUSTINES
SPICED PORK BELLY
WINES
WHITE WINES
SAUVIGNON BLANC
PINOT GRIGIO
CHARDONNAY
CHARDONNAY/VIOGNIER
SANCERRE
ESTATE CHARDONNAY
CHASSAGNE-MONTRACHET
BÂTARD-MONTRACHET GRAND CRU
RED WINES
MERLOT
RIOJA
SHIRAZ VAT 8
SYRAH
ESTATE SHIRAZ VIOGNIER
PINOT NOIR
CHÂTEAU LA TOUR HAUT-BRION
2004 CLOS DE LA ROCHE
CHAMPAGNES
PERRIER-JOUËT GRAND BRUT NV
BOLLINGER SPECIAL CUVEE NV
PERRIER-JOUËT BLASON ROSE
BOLLINGER VINTAGE 2000
KRUG GRAND CUVEE
PERRIER-JOUËT BELLE ÉPOQUE MAGNUM

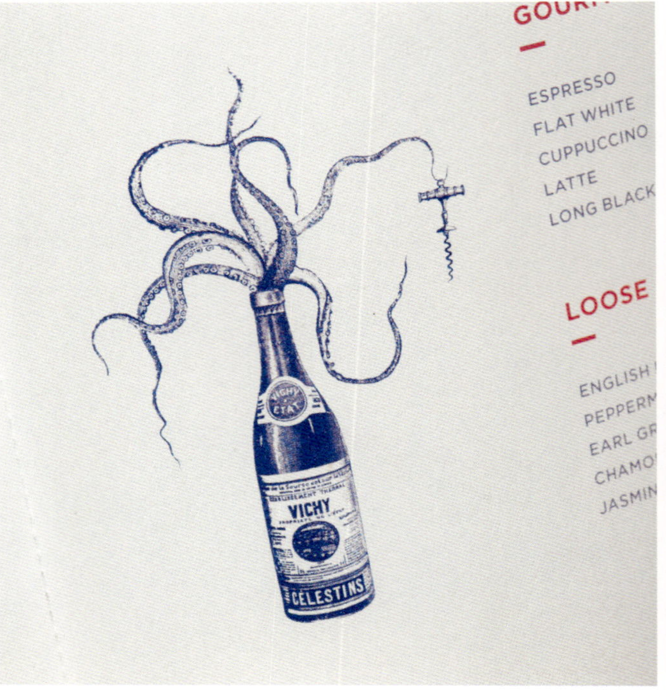

Pelican

The Pelican is a seafood dining institute inspired by the comfort and celebratory spirit of seafarers returning to land after a long voyage. Inspired by the pelican, a bird often seen in coastal regions, the restaurant brings to mind the anticipation of visiting a brief haven, where the comforts of good food and great company reside. The graphic mixing human characters interacting with sea-like animals is inspired by the dual functions of the Pelican restaurant and bar. As the evening progresses, The Pelican transforms from a dining space into a groovy wine bar and club, lasting deep into the night. This blurring of the boundary between when it is a restaurant and when it becomes a bar, is a blurring of what is formal and what is not; leading to the graphical interpretation of blurring the boundary between what is real and what is imaginary. As the boundary blurs, the graphic expression then goes into a series of illustrations that features a Mary Poppins-like character riding a giant pelican, or playing sea-horse jockey. The same design intent is communicated within the interior space design through the neon pink sea-horse sporting a diver's mask, or singular tear-drop light fixtures suspended in air.

Design Agency: Foreign Policy Design Group | Creative Direction: Yah-Leng Yu | Art Direction: Yah-Leng Yu | Design: May Lim

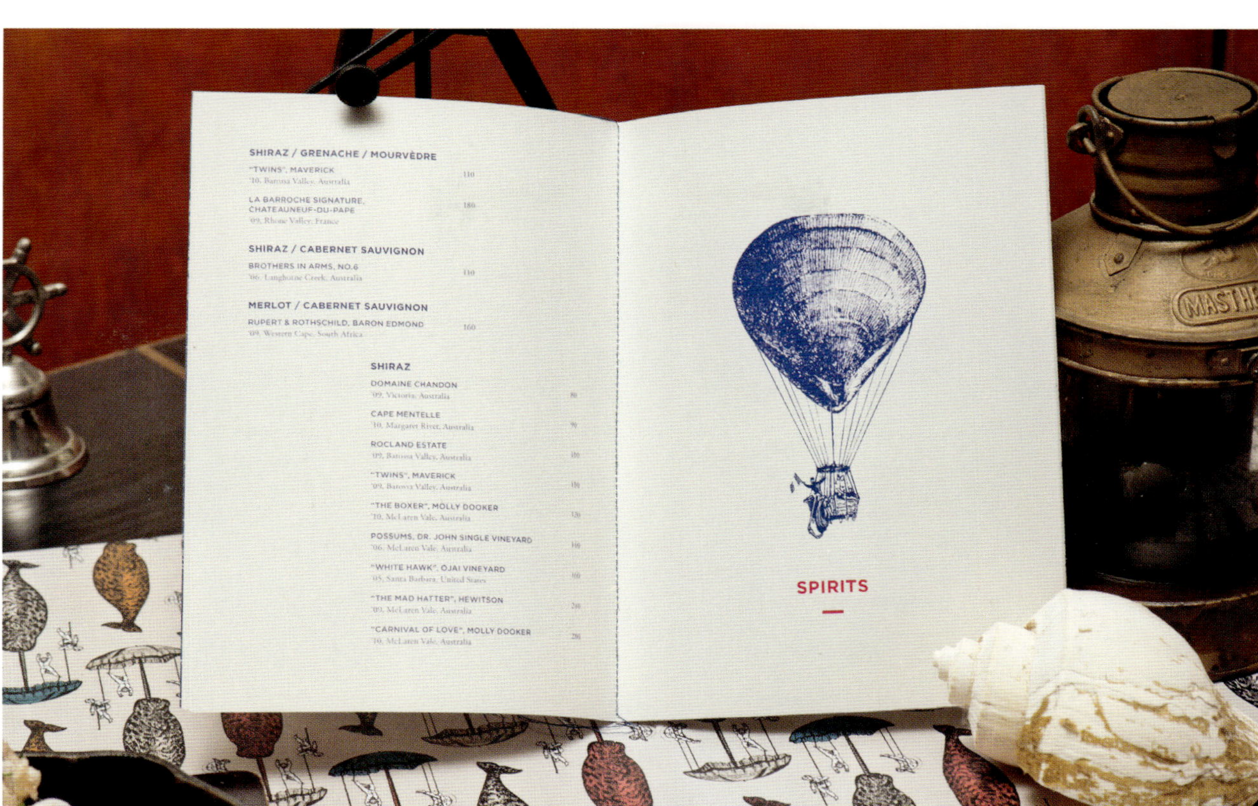

SHIRAZ / GRENACHE / MOURVÈDRE
"TWINS", MAVERICK
LA BARROCHE SIGNATURE, CHATEAUNEUF-DU-PAPE
SHIRAZ / CABERNET SAUVIGNON
BROTHERS IN ARMS, NO.6
MERLOT / CABERNET SAUVIGNON
RUPERT & ROTHSCHILD, BARON EDMOND
SHIRAZ
DOMAINE CHANDON
CAPE MENTELLE
ROCLAND ESTATE
"TWINS", MAVERICK
"THE BOXER", MOLLY DOOKER
POSSUMS, DR. JOHN SINGLE VINEYARD
"WHITE HAWK", OJAI VINEYARD
"THE MAD HATTER", HEWITSON
"CARNIVAL OF LOVE", MOLLY DOOKER
SPIRITS

Avalanche Print

Avalanche Print is an online platform offering a choice of silk printed tote bags as well as silk printed notebooks.

There is a range of 7 models and 5 colors to choose from. Every item is silk printed one by one, and the project's whole idea is to highlight the process of hand-made silk print and to make it popular again.

Client: Avalanche Print | Design Agency: Say What Studio | Photography: Pierre-Luc Baron-Moreau

AVALANCHE
COTTON TOTE BAG
SILK PRINTED
ONE
N
PRODUCT DESCRIPTION
NEVERLAND
FINISHED PRINTING ON 19 / 06 / 12 AT 7 00 AM PM
SIZE: ONE SIZE / 420 x 380mm / 330mm HANDLES
COMPOSITION: 100% NATURAL COTTON / 110g / BIODEGRADABLE
SILK PRINT COLOR: BLACK BLUE RED GOLD PEACOCK
CARE: MACHINE WASH MAX 30°C / IRON AT 100° MAX / DO NOT BLEACH
THE AVALANCHE TOTE BAGS AS WELL AS THEIR TAGS AND PACKAGING ARE CAREFULLY SILK-PRINTED BY HAND. EACH MODEL IS AVAILABLE IN A RANGE OF COLORS, ALLOWING YOU TO CHOOSE ACCORDING TO YOUR PREFERENCES. SENT STRAIGHT TO YOU AND READY TO USE!
WWW.AVALANCHE-PRINT.COM
XII
YOU'VE GOT MAIL
RECIPIENT
ADDRESS
ZIP CODE
CITY
COUNTRY
MANUFACTURED, PACKAGED AND SENT BY AVALANCHE PRINT

AVALANCHE
ONE
N
ONE

AVALANCHE
COTTON TOTE BAG
DEUS EX MACHINA
AVALANCHE PRINT
PRODUCT DESCRIPTION
YOU'VE GOT MAIL

Las Buenas Maneras

Using just a blue rollerball pen and some watercolors, Las Buenas Maneras in Medellín, Columbia comes to life and is inspired by antique ceramics, and the romantic concept of returning to the time of good manners and etiquette at the table. Vintage spoons and traditional plates, combined with tips and tricks to behave at the table are used across the packaging material and stationery. Rubber stamps with the logotype have also been incorporated to give a handmade well-worn final look.

Client: Las Buenas Maneras | Design Agency: Wallnut

Las
BUENAS
Maneras
-1853-

Las
BUENAS
Maneras
-1853-

The Wishing Chair

Branding development for decor store, Delhi, India.

Client: Delhi | Design Agency: Wallnut

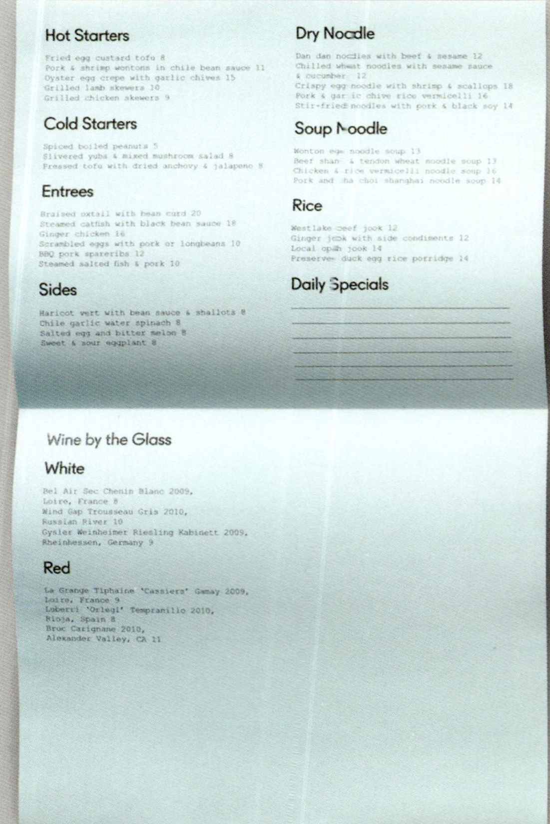

Hot Starters

Fried egg custard tofu 8
Pork & shrimp wontons in chile bean sauce 11
Oyster egg crepe with garlic chives 15
Grilled lamb skewers 10
Grilled chicken skewers 9

Cold Starters

Spiced boiled peanuts 5
Slivered yuba & mixed mushroom salad 8
Pressed tofu with dried anchovy & jalapeno 8

Entrees

Braised oxtail with bean curd 20
Steamed catfish with black bean sauce 18
Ginger chicken 16
Scrambled eggs with pork or longbeans 10
BBQ pork spareribs 12
Steamed salted fish & pork 10

Sides

Haricot vert with bean sauce & shallots 8
Chile garlic water spinach 8
Salted egg and bitter melon 8
Sweet & sour eggplant 8

Dry Noodle

Dan dan noodles with beef & sesame 12
Chilled wheat noodles with sesame sauce & cucumber 12
Crispy egg noodle with shrimp & scallops 18
Pork & garlic chive rice vermicelli 16
Stir-fried noodles with pork & black soy 14

Soup Noodle

Wonton egg noodle soup 13
Beef shank & tendon wheat noodle soup 13
Chicken & rice vermicelli noodle soup 16
Pork and cha choi shanghai noodle soup 14

Rice

Westlake beef jook 12
Ginger jook with side condiments 12
Local opah jook 14
Preserved duck egg rice porridge 14

Daily Specials

Wine by the Glass

White

Bel Air Sec Chenin Blanc 2009,
Loire, France 8
Wind Gap Trousseau Gris 2010,
Russian River 10
Gysler Weinheimer Riesling Kabinett 2009,
Rheinhessen, Germany 9

Red

La Grange Tiphaine 'Cassiers' Gamay 2009,
Loire, France 9
Luberri 'Orlegi' Tempranillo 2010,
Rioja, Spain 8
Broc Carignane 2010,
Alexander Valley, CA 11

Wo Hing General Store

Wo Hing General Store is a contemporary restaurant in San Francisco's Mission district presenting a unique take on Chinese street-food. The identity references the delicate nature of noodles, a main staple on the restaurant's menu. In addition to the logo, Manual created a rich, colorful visual language using only the aforementioned humble noodle. Using a scanner, designers experimented with raw and cooked noodles to create a number of flowing, abstract images. As a departure from the ubiquitous neon sign seen in many Chinese restaurants, Manual designed a lightweight transparent window sign, screen printed with electroluminescent ink.

Client: Wo Hing General Store | Design Agency: Manual | Creative Direction: Tom Crabtree | Design: Tom Crabtree, Dante Iniguez, Eileen Lee | Photography: Manual

Materello

Materello is a gastronomical company that specializes in Authentic Italian Food. Materello presents a new packaging concept for pasta: more visually appealing, and easier to maintain and store. The packaging has been fabricated with tubes and lids that already exist in the market. The variety of pasta are easily differentiated by the colors and the different illustrations.

The simple logo and series of illustrations combine with a clean and simple design, which emphasizes the quality of the product.

Design: Sonia Castillo

authentic italian food
M
materello

authentic italian food
M
materello

authentic italian food
M
materello

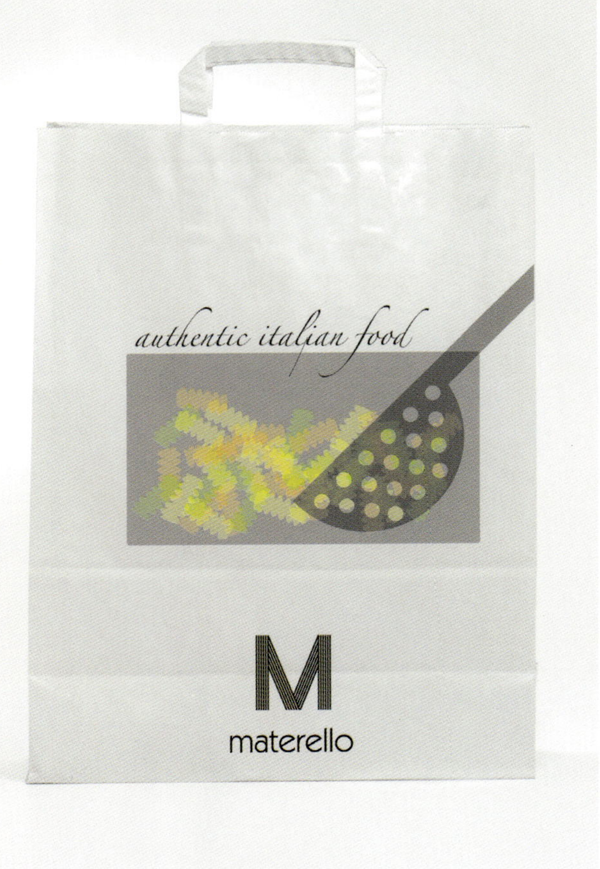
authentic italian food
M
materello

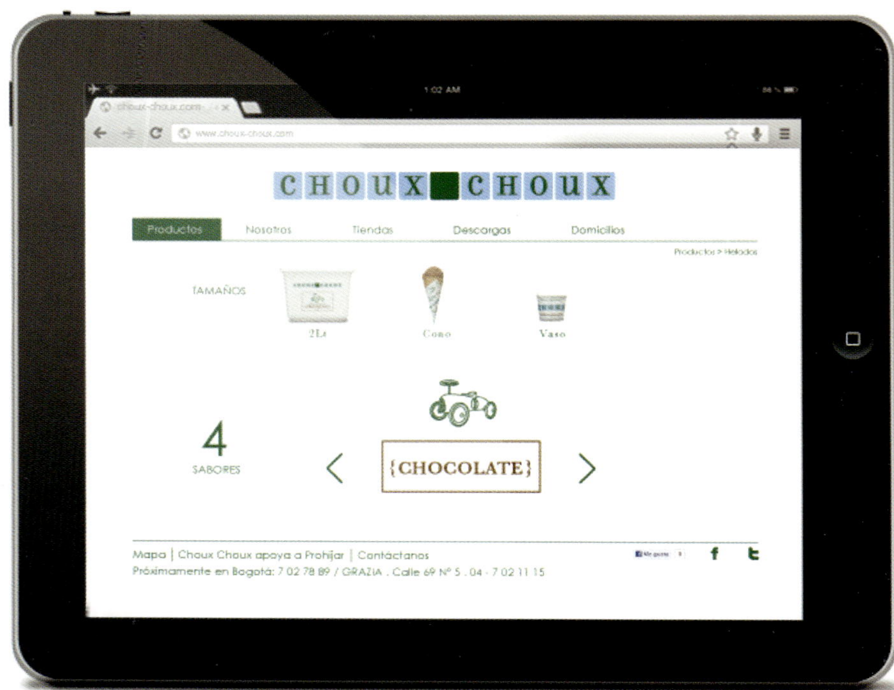

Choux Choux

The clients desire for this ice cream brand was to give people a break, and allow them to play or rest. To achieve this, P576 suggested 4 of the clients write a list about how they played, or toys they played with in their childhood. In addition, the client wanted to communicate through the design the care that went into choosing ingredients, and the traditional way the ice cream is prepared. The solution was in the design style: symmetrical and simple images that connote rigor, mixed with monochromatic illustrations that help connect with the past.

Client: Choux Choux | Design Agency: P576 | Creative Direction: Arutza Rico Onzaga | Design: María Silva, Felipe Osorio | Illustration: Angélica del Valle, Felipe Osorio | Photgraphy: Javier Ramírez, Lucho Mariño.

HELADO ARTESANAL
{CHOCOLATE}
2 L

HELADO ARTESANAL
{VAINILLA}
2 L

SORBETE ARTESANAL
{MANGO & LIMÓN}
2 L

{CHOCOLATE}
{CHOCOLATE}
{AREQUIPE}

INGREDIENTES
LECHE ENTERA
CREMA DE LECHE
YEMA DE HUEVO
AZÚCAR
SABORES NATURALES SEGÚN DENOMINACIÓN DE LA ETIQUETA.
PUEDE CONTENER NUECES.
CHOUX-CHOUX.COM

INGREDIENTES
AGUA MINERAL
AZÚCAR
PULPA DE FRUTA
LA FRUTA SEGÚN DENOMINACIÓN DE LA ETIQUETA.
PUEDE CONTENER NUECES.
CHOUX-CHOUX.COM

CHOUX CHOUX
HELADO ARTESANAL
{CHOCOLATE}
2 L

INGREDIENTES
LECHE ENTERA
CREMA DE LECHE
YEMA DE HUEVO
AZÚCAR
SABORES NATURALES SEGÚN DENOMINACIÓN DE LA ETIQUETA.
PUEDE CONTENER NUECES.
CHOUX-CHOUX.COM

INGREDIENTES
LECHE ENTERA
CREMA DE LECHE
YEMA DE HUEVO
AZÚCAR
SABORES NATURALES SEGÚN DENOMINACIÓN DE LA ETIQUETA.
PUEDE CONTENER NUECES.
CHOUX-CHOUX.COM

INGREDIENTES
LECHE ENTERA
CREMA DE LECHE
YEMA DE HUEVO
AZÚCAR
SABORES NATURALES SEGÚN DENOMINACIÓN DE LA ETIQUETA.
PUEDE CONTENER NUECES.
CHOUX-CHOUX.COM

INGREDIENTES
LECHE ENTERA
CREMA DE LECHE
YEMA DE HUEVO
AZÚCAR
SABORES NATURALES SEGÚN DENOMINACIÓN DE LA ETIQUETA.
PUEDE CONTENER NUECES.
CHOUX-CHOUX.COM

The Chain Reaction Project

The Chain Reaction Project (TCRP) is a non-profit organization that was born in 2009 to help change lives in some of the world's least-developed nations. TCRP's mission is to find a cause, have an effect, and from there, grow their initiative by inspiring others to be catalysts for change as well.

Client: The Chain Reaction Project | Design Agency: Bravo Company | Creative Direction: Edwin Tan | Art Direction: Amanda Ho, Pharaon Siraj

charity

hiking

environment

animal rights

nature

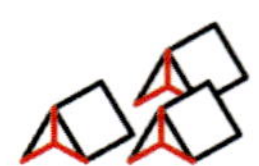

disaster relief

the arts

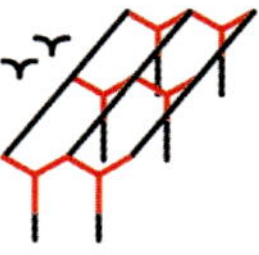

infrastructure

disability

human rights

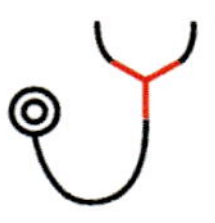

medical access

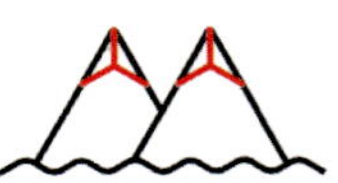

mountaineering

cycling

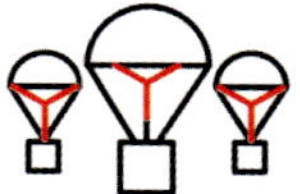

war-related aid

sustainable energy

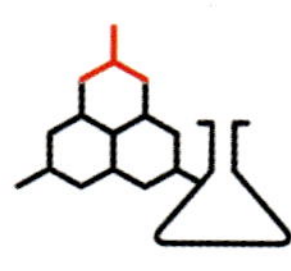

scientific research

education

logistics

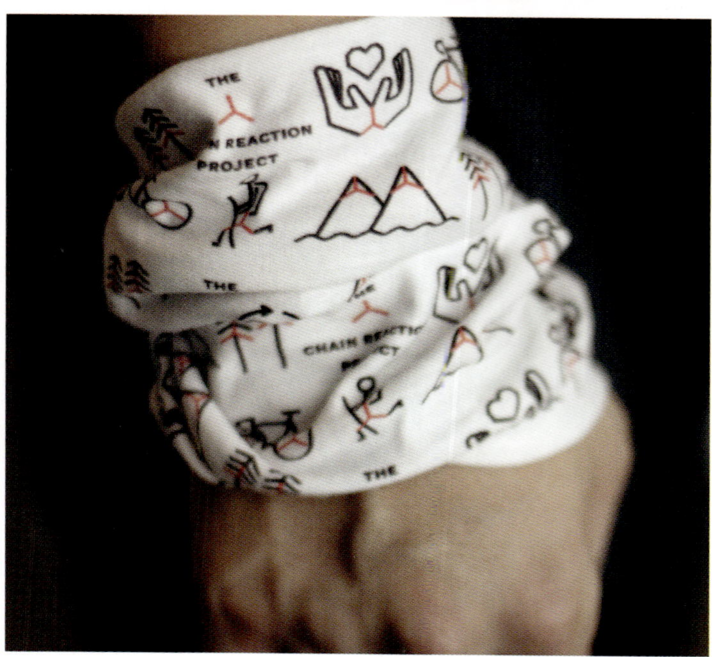

Miniclub

Miniclub is an electronic music club located in Valencia, Spain. Every weekend there is a different international DJ playing in the club. As a result of its extensive program, Miniclub was decided to create monthly and weekly flyers and posters to communicate this message. To this end, the illustration was used to create a big visual impact, to communicate the unique personality of the club, and to differentiate itself from the rest of clubs located this area of the country.

Client: Grupo Hossegor | Creative Direction: Antonio Ladrillo | Design: Antonio Ladrillo | Illustration: Antonio Ladrillo

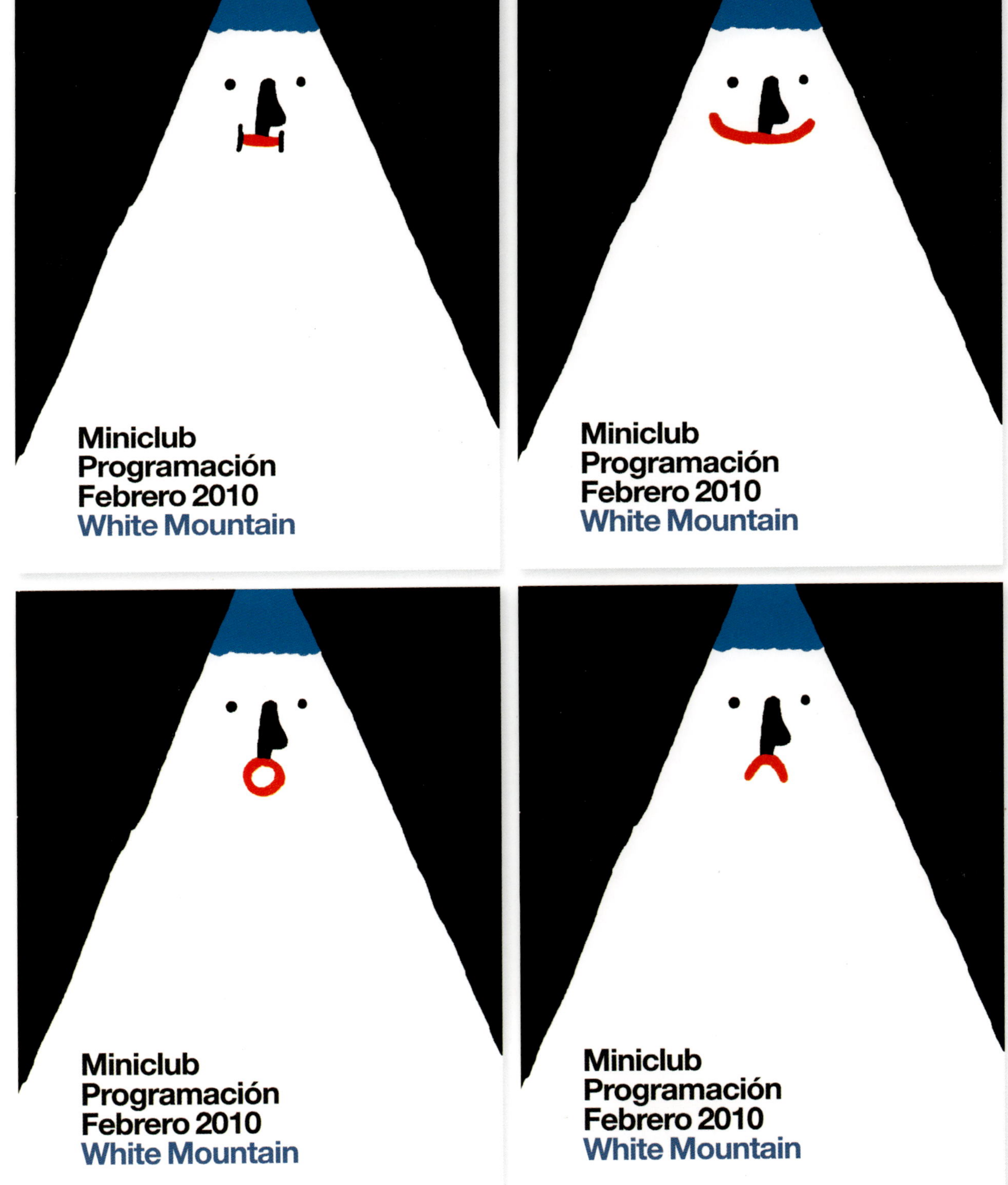

Victory

Olive oil is a widespread product in France. We are used to consuming olive oil from the Mediterranean region, while olive oil from Japan is still a relatively unknown product. In Japan, olive oil is a symbol for victory, and success at school and work. It also represents success in love and war.

The olive tree is the Tree of Life.

Client: Victory | Design: Arthur Foliard

Flowergala

Over the past 35 years, Polytrade Paper Corporation has been introducing different overseas paper brands, and innovative paper uses to markets and users. This time, Polytrade brought us Astrobrights papers, which come in 23 bright colors and attracts people's attention. To launch this new paper series, Polytrade held a launch party in a restaurant in Macau, China. BLOW were asked to create the event name, identity, promotional materials, and decoration for the event.

Client: Polytrade Paper Corporation Limited | Design Agency: BLOW | Designer: Ken Lo, Crystal Cheung, Caspar Ip | Copywriter: Ken Lo

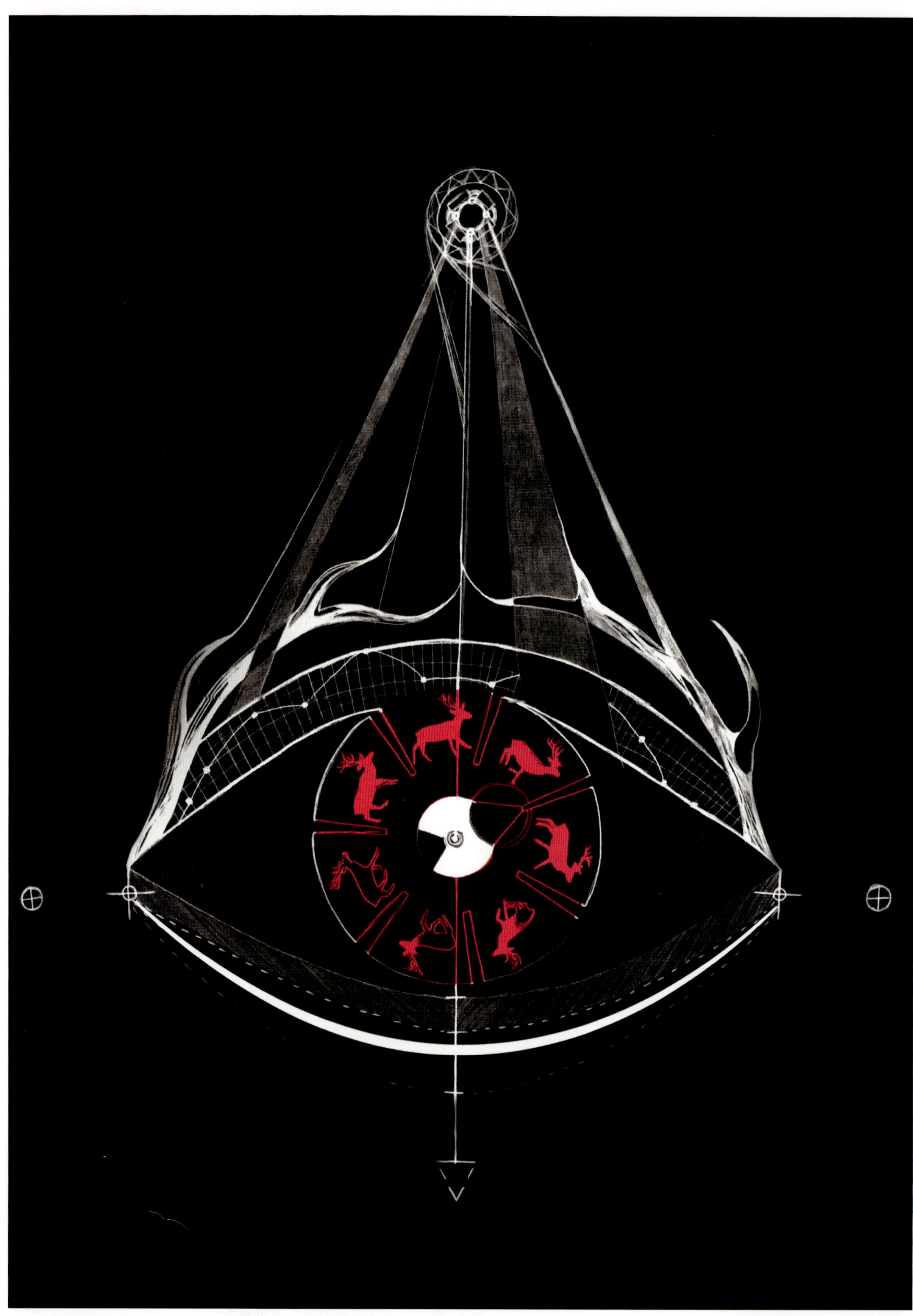

Drink Up UTS

A series of 6 wine labels for the UTS School of Design. Each label represents the 6 disciplines of design through illustrated versions of the third eye. The concept being, we are all born with a third eye, or "inner eye," but we must learn to open it through the course of our lives to reach the highest levels of creativity.

Client: UTS | Design: Bec Kilpatrick

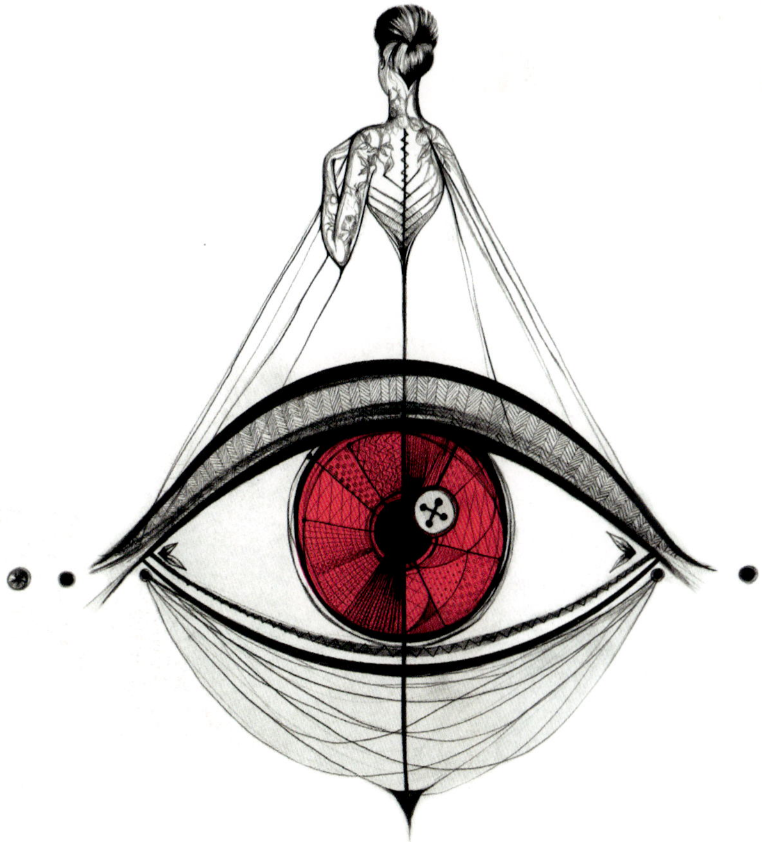

cake
create. culture.
CHARDONNAY
750mL

cake
create. culture.
CHARDONNAY
750mL

cake
create. culture.
CHARDONNAY
750mL
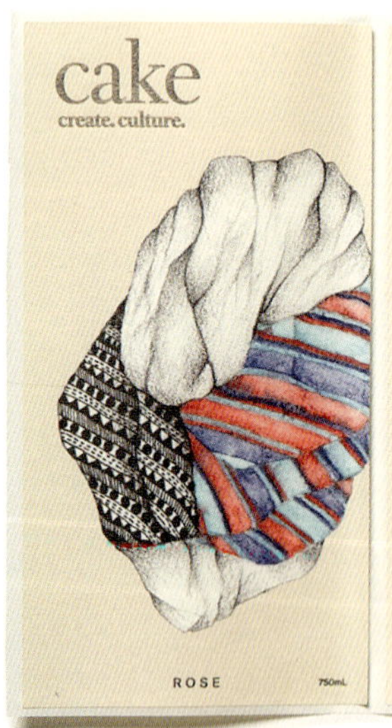
cake
create. culture.
ROSE
750mL
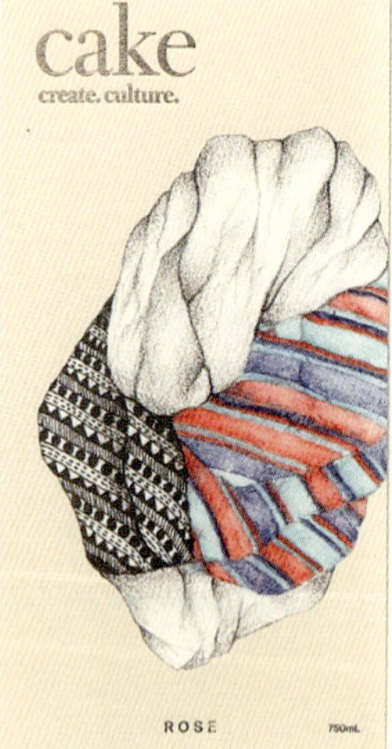
cake
create. culture.
ROSE
750mL
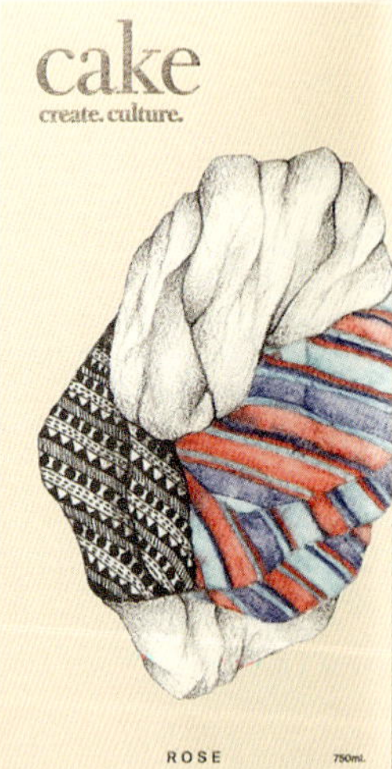
cake
create. culture.
ROSE
750mL
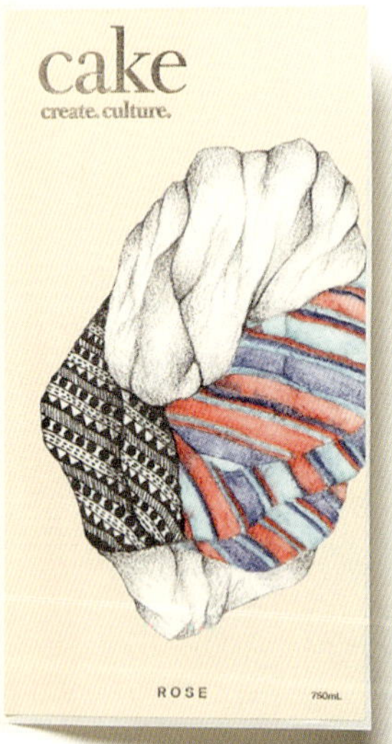
cake
create. culture.
ROSE
750mL
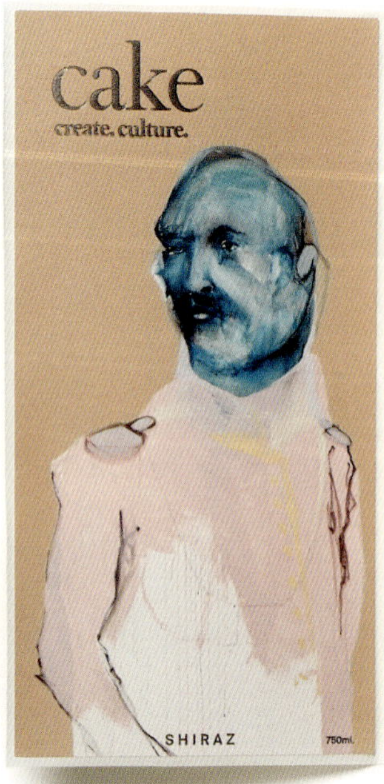
cake
create. culture.
SHIRAZ
750mL

cake
create. culture.
SHIRAZ
750mL

cake
create. culture.
SHIRAZ
750mL

Cake Wines New Range

Cake Wines released a new range, adding a Shiraz, Chardonnay, and Rose to the collection. Zé Studio worked to bring the art to life through considered typography, layout, and printing techniques including foiling and Cake Wines embellishments.

Client: Cake Wines | Design Agency: Zé Studio | Artists/Illustrations: Daniel (Ears) O'toole (Shiraz), Jae Copp (Chardonnay), Manuela Strano (Rosé), Mark Whalen (Cabernet Merlot), Beci Orpin (Sauvignon Blanc), Kevin Tran (Pinot Noir), Hollie Martin (Pinot Grigio)

Strong Nutrients

Pearlfisher has created the brand strategy, naming, identity, packaging, retail, and digital communications for Strong, a range of high quality complex nutrients.

The new design creates a powerful visual story using the metaphor of beautiful and elegant birds that have hidden strength. The brand name – Strong – and the playful variant names and descriptors are simple yet impactful, and clearly communicate the brand's promise of inner strength and outer beauty.

Client: Strong Nutrients | Design Agency: Pearlfisher | Creative Direction: Karen Welman | Art Direction: Karen Welman | Illustration: Andy Lyons

Strong
chill pill
Strong
sunshine pill
Strong
Antarctic krill
Strong
brain box
30caps

Jose Gourmet Canned Goods

These are typical Portuguese canned goods, despite not having the traditional aspect that we are used to. Meet the brand Jose Gourmet, born from the friendship of an airplane pilot (Adriano Ribeiro) and a designer/illustrator (Luís Mendonça). The challenge was to reach a target audience of both children and adults, and put aside the nostalgic aesthetics usually associated with the canned goods industry by picking prestigious Portuguese illustrators. They also invited a well known Portuguese chef, who created recipes for children – emphasizing simplicity and fun – and also to adults – with a more sophisticated confection, and new exquisite flavors. The writer Eugénio Rodas developed micro narratives that associate the specific characteristics of the product with the imaginary.

Client: Jose Gourmet | Design: Luís Mendonça | Illustration: Gémeo Luís, André Letria, Bernardo Carvalho, Cristina Valadas, Emílio Remelhe, Francisco Providência, Inês Oliveira, João Machado, João V.Carvalho, Madalena Matoso, Rui Mendonça, Teresa Lima, Tiago Manuel, Yara Kono | Photography: Pedro Reis

SARDINHAS "PETINGAS" EM TOMATE
SMALL SARDINES IN TOMATO SAUCE
PETITES SARDINES À LA TOMATE
PRODUTO DE PORTUGAL . PRODUCT OF PORTUGAL . PRODUIT DU PORTUGAL
LOTE CONSUMIR DE PREFERÊNCIA ANTES DE
LOT BEST BEFORE
SARDINHAS "PETINGAS" PICANTES
SPICED SMALL SARDINES
PETITES SARDINES PIQUANTES
SARDINHAS EM AZEITE EXTRA VIRGEM BIOLÓGICO
SARDINES IN BIOLOGIC EXTRA VIRGIN OLIVE OIL
SARDINES À L'HUILE D'OLIVE VIERGE EXTRA BIOLOGIQUE
WWW.JOSEGOURMET.COM
CARAPAUZINHOS EM MOLHO DE ESCABECHE
STICKLEBACK IN PICKLED SAUCE
ÉPINOCHES EN SAUCE MARINADE
SARDINHAS EM AZEITE COM LIMÃO
SARDINES IN OLIVE OIL WITH LEMON
SARDINES À L'HUILE D'OLIVE ET CITRON
FILETES DE CAVALA EM AZEITE
MACKEREL FILLETS IN OLIVE OIL
FILETS DE MAQUEREAUX À L'HUILE D'OLIVE
VENTRESCA DE ATUM EM AZEITE
VENTRESCA DE ATUM EM AZEITE
VENTRESCA DE ATUM EM AZEITE

Tjuvholmen Sjømagasin

Identity, branding, graphic design, illustration/art, and environmental design for a seafood restaurant in Oslo, Norway. It is situated at Tjuvholmen, a waterfront area in central Oslo. The specialty of the restaurant is grilled seafood, and the wood–fire grill burns at a constant temperature, with the wood giving the food a tender, smoked flavor. Tjuvholmen Sjømagasin is divided into several areas, so that each department operates individually. The restaurant consists of the main restaurant, the Seafood Bar, the Chambre Separée, the Mezzanine, the Fish Deli, and the Conference Center.

Client: Fursetgruppen | Design Agency: Work in Progress | Design: Torgeir Hjetland | Illustration: Torgeir Hjetland, Jan T. Rafdal

Takk for besøket
sjømagasin

Bar Noire

Enter the deep dark world of Bar Noire for a relaxing glass of wine, and exquisite tapas. Let the wonderfully sinister array of creatures seduce you as they dance around the walls leading you through the underground passageways and into private, ambient lit booths. Located in the depths of Surry Hills Sydney, this new establishment is the perfect place for an after work hangout or weekend catch-up.

Client: Bar Noire | Design: Bec Kilpatrick

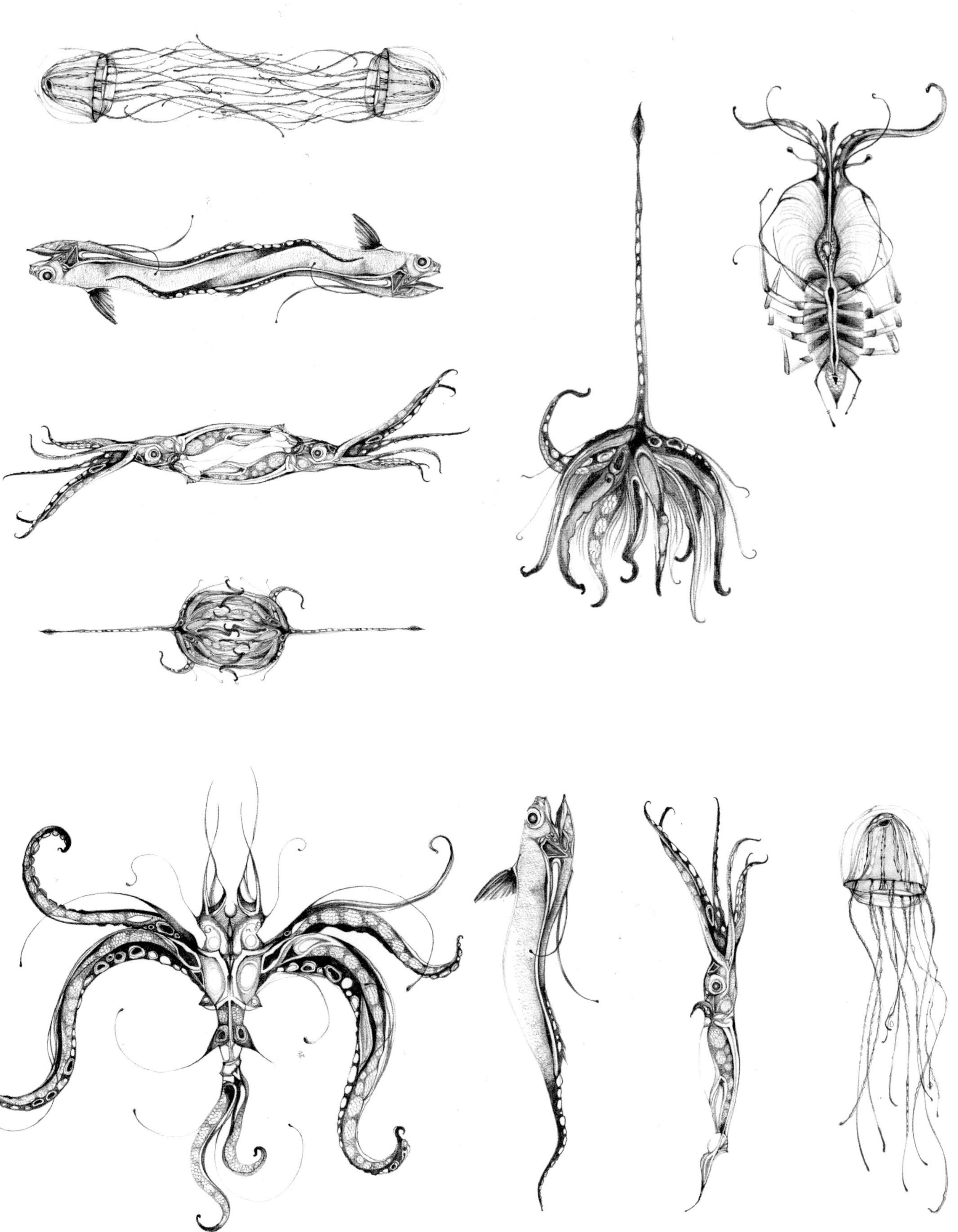

Bib & Tucker

Bib & Tucker is a restaurant and bar on Leighton Beach in Fremantle, Western Australian and is the latest venture by Olympic swimmer Eamon Sullivan. End of Work were given the name and an empty, fairly non-descript white box situated on the beach. End of Work invented a back-story around two dandified bandits – Bib and Tucker – an early Australian version of Bonnie and Clyde. The story goes that they would have been just as likely to compliment you on your exquisite taste in shoes as to relieve you of your wallet. This theme of "elegant rascality" set the tone for the project, and working with Romy Alwill and Will Dangar, End of Work utilized a stripped-back color palette, and tactile rustic materials to build a brand with grit, authenticity, and a tiny splash of elegance.

Client: Bib & Tucker | Design Agency: End of Work

BIB & TUCKER
BIB AND TUCKER —
20 Leighton Beach Bvd.
Nth. Fremantle W.A. 6159
T. 08 9431 2147
info@bibandtucker.net.au
BIBANDTUCKER.NET.AU

Tokio Restaurant

Tokio is not only one of the best sushi restaurants in Budapest, it also becomes a hip and fancy cocktail bar at night, with excellent DJs. You can enjoy a delicious ramen, miso, and tiger-crayfish tempura for a great business lunch, or you can have a cocktail with wasabi and jasmine after work.

The bent neon signs are based on the handwriting of one of the owners. The main wall is an imaginary detail of the Shibuya District of Tokyo. On the other wall, a big iconic robot appears like a huge guardian of the restaurant. The signs for the toilets are made from enamel at the biggest enamel factory in Hungary.

The logo is based on the Japanese sign for Tokyo City. A small play with the letters made the typography more authentic but still readable. The key visual element of the restaurant is the robot, holding sushi and chopsticks in its hands. We can find the robot in the menu, and on the manually spray painted flyers as well.

Client: Tokio Restaurant | Interior Design: Viktor Csap | Design: Eszter Laki | Copywriter: Vera Vida | Illustration: Eszter Laki | Photography: Balázs Glódi

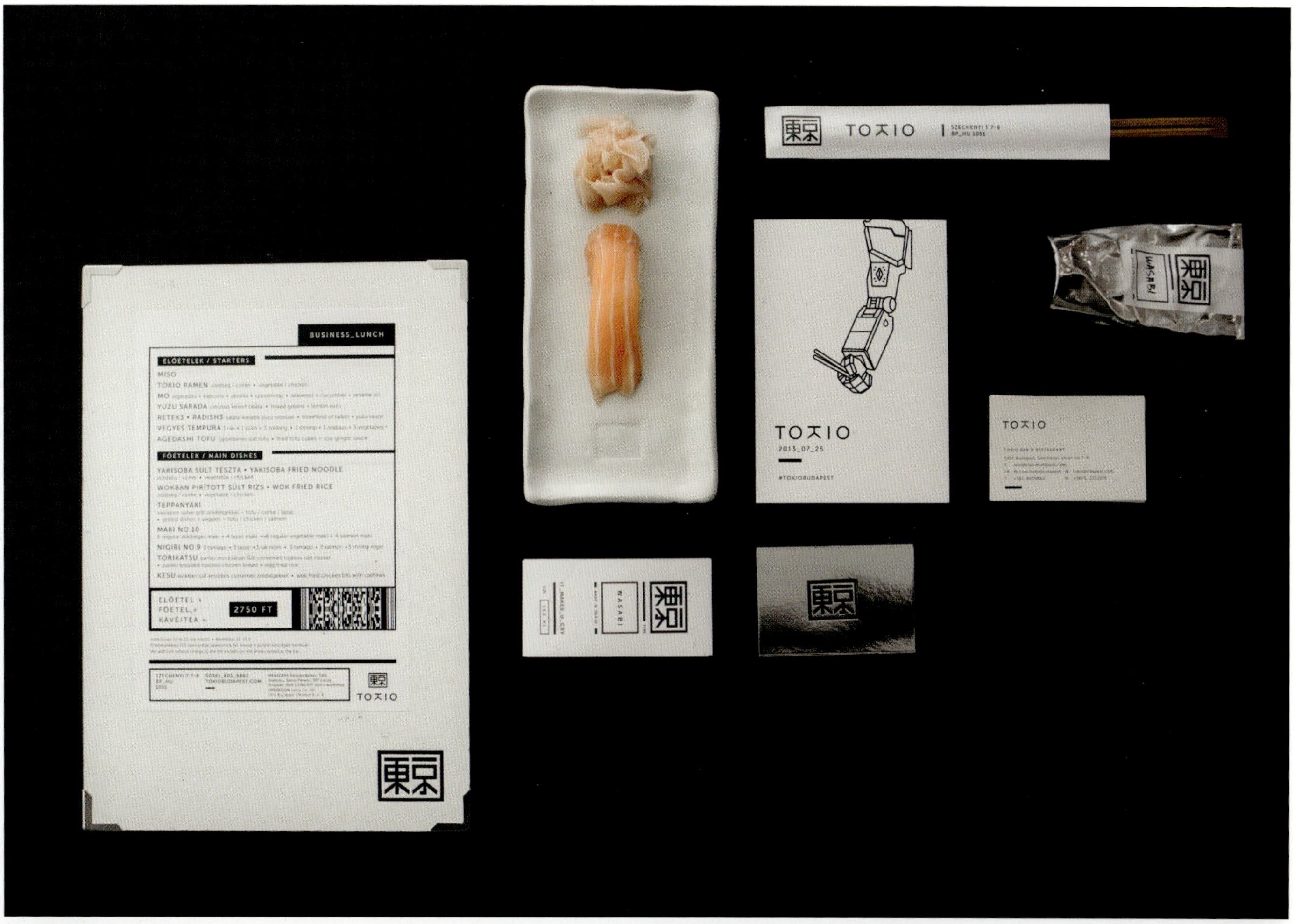
BUSINESS_LUNCH
ELŐÉTELEK / STARTERS
FŐÉTELEK / MAIN DISHES
2750 FT
TOKIO
2013_07_25
#TOKIOBUDAPEST
WASABI

STEP NO 3.
もう一本のはしを下のはしとして
親指のつけ根と薬指ではさむ。
STEP NO 4.
上のはしだけを動かすように
下のはしは動かさない。

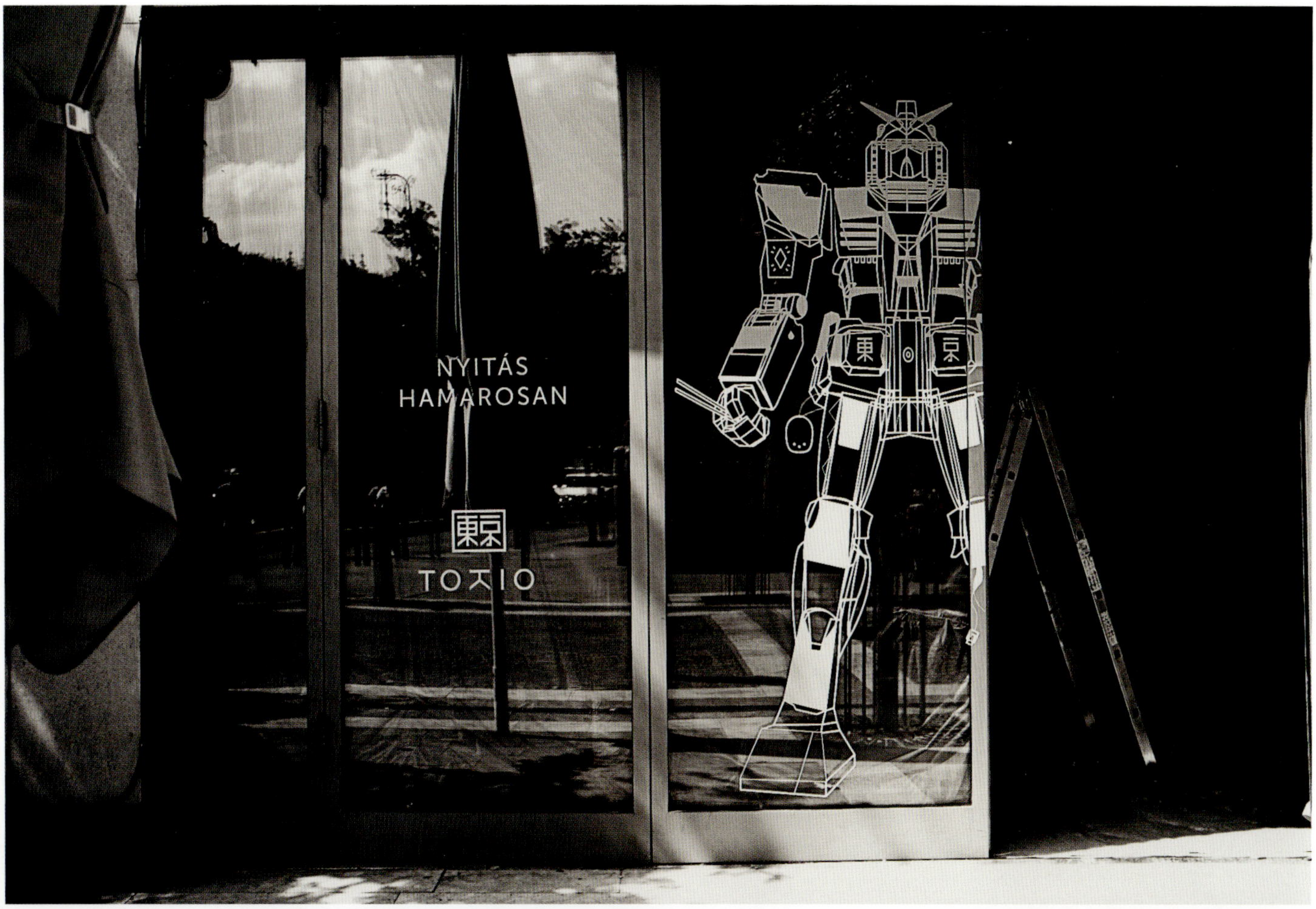
NYITÁS
HAMAROSAN
TOKIO

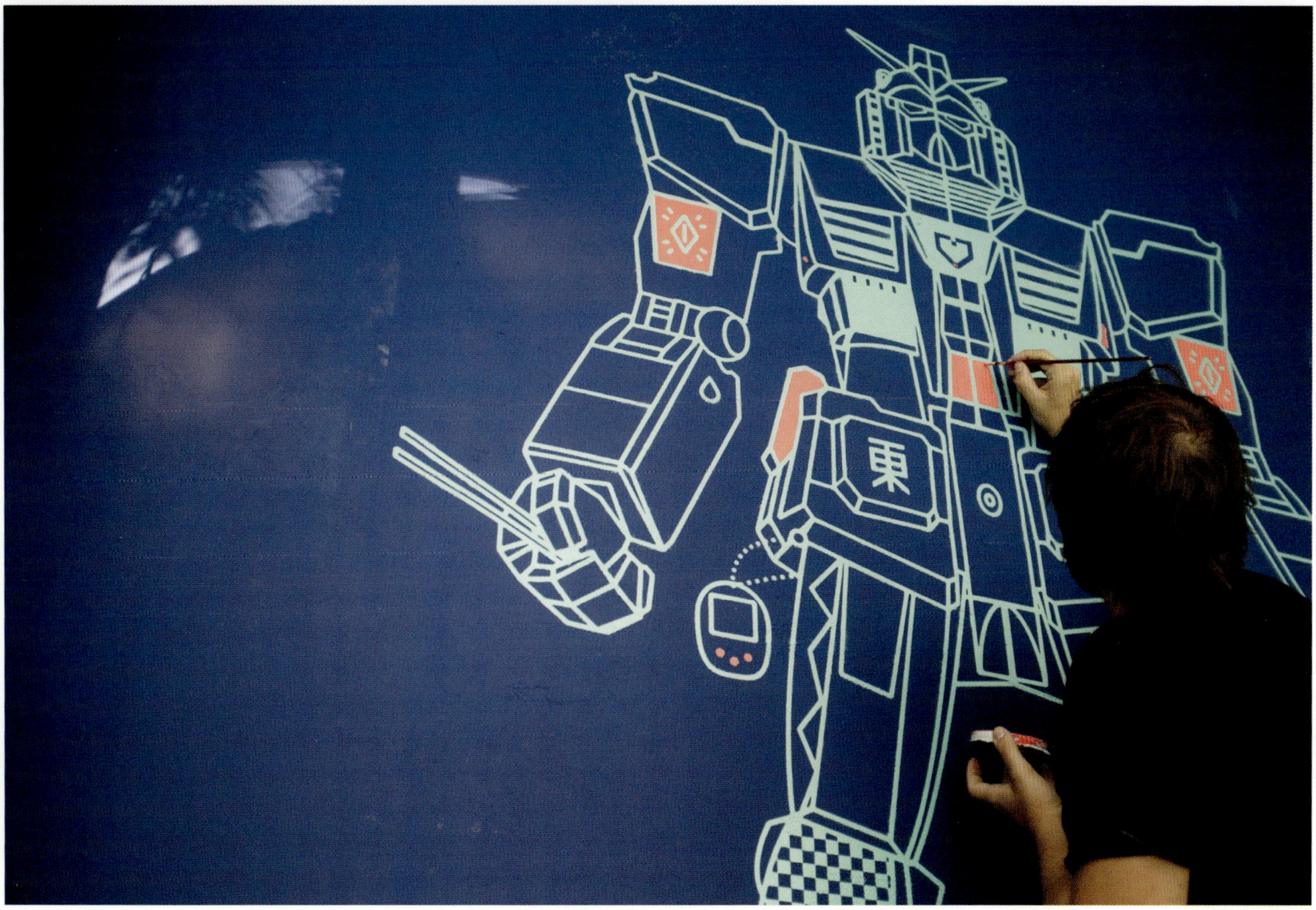

It Takes Four Sorts

Visual Identity for "It Takes Four Sorts" – Art Exchange among Mainland China, Taiwan, Hong Kong, and Macao 2012.

Client: Osage Art Foundation | Design Agency: DESIGNER+ARTIST

香港 Hong Kong
深圳 Shenzhen
臺灣 Taiwan
澳門 Macau
It Takes Four Sorts
Art Exchange among Mainland China, Taiwan, Hong Kong and Macao 2012
臺灣 2012.5.19 — 7.15
臺北市立美術館 展覽室3C
Taipei Fine Arts Museum Gallery 3C
香港 2012.9.14 — 10.14
香港奧沙藝術中心
Osage Gallery
澳門 2012.8.3 — 9.2
南灣舊法院大樓
Old Court Building in South Bay
深圳 2012.10.21 — 11.18
何香凝美術館
Hexiangning art museum
臺北市立美術館
TAIPEI FINE ARTS MUSEUM

香港 Hong Kong
深圳 Shenzhen
臺灣 Taiwan
澳門 Macau
It Takes Four Sorts
Art Exchange among Mainland China, Taiwan, Hong Kong and Macao 2012
臺灣 2012.5.19 — 7.15
臺北市立美術館 展覽室3C
香港 2012.9.14 — 10.14
香港奧沙藝術中心
澳門 2012.8.3 — 9.2
南灣舊法院大樓
深圳 2012.10.21 — 11.18
何香凝美術館
臺北市立美術館
TAIPEI FINE ARTS MUSEUM

香港 Hong Kong
深圳 Shenzhen
臺灣 Taiwan
澳門 Macau
It Takes Four Sorts
Art Exchange among Mainland China, Taiwan, Hong Kong and Macao 2012
臺灣 2012.5.19 — 7.15
臺北市立美術館 展覽室3C
香港 2012.9.14 — 10.14
香港奧沙藝術中心
澳門 2012.8.3 — 9.2
南灣舊法院大樓
深圳 2012.10.21 — 11.18
何香凝美術館
臺北市立美術館
TAIPEI FINE ARTS MUSEUM

香港 Hong Kong
深圳 Shenzhen
臺灣 Taiwan
澳門 Macau
It Takes Four Sorts
Art Exchange among Mainland China, Taiwan, Hong Kong and Macao 2012
臺灣 2012.5.19 — 7.15
臺北市立美術館 展覽室3C
香港 2012.9.14 — 10.14
香港奧沙藝術中心
澳門 2012.8.3 — 9.2
南灣舊法院大樓
深圳 2012.10.21 — 11.18
何香凝美術館
臺北市立美術館
TAIPEI FINE ARTS MUSEUM

Meat & Bakery TAVERN

In store poster for “Meat & Bakery TAVERN,” a Brooklyn themed bakery/restaurant that offers meat dishes and homemade bread. In designing the poster, a classic and valuable feel was implemented to match the interior. The poster was designed utilizing images of meats, and the names of variou parts. For the names of breads, classic fonts were adopted. In terms of expressing material value, the posters were printed implementing letter pressing (relief printing), and silkscreen (superior in color emphasis) printing.

By visualizing the restaurant concept for visiting customers, the atmosphere of the space, and the cuisines (materials) offered were clarified. Furthermore, a limited sale of the posters sold out despite their high costs.

Client: Conception Co.,Ltd. | Design Agency: AD&D | Creative Direction: Ren Takaya | Art Direction: Ren Takaya | Design: Ren Takaya, Shunryo Yamanaka | Copywriter: Rika Takaya | Illustration: Mao Nishida | Photography: Masayoshi Harabuchi

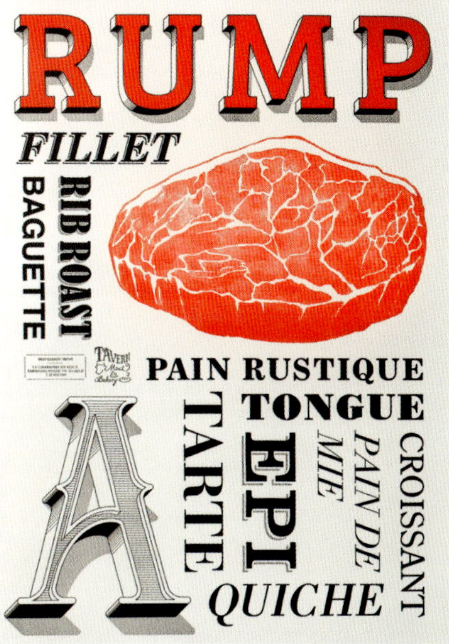

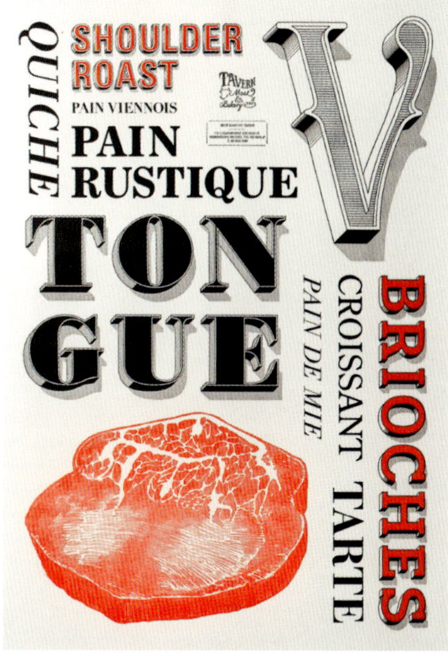

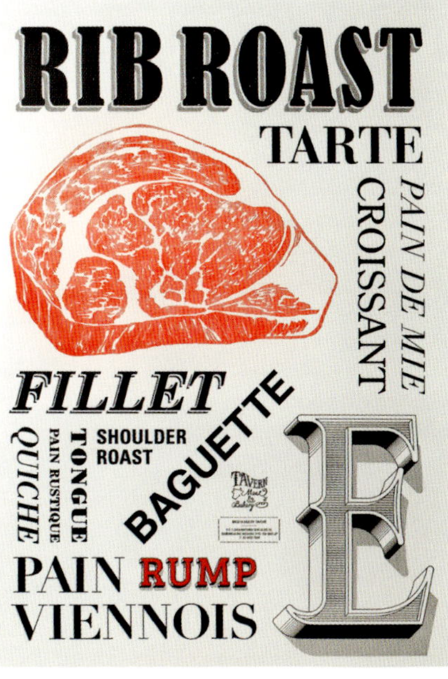

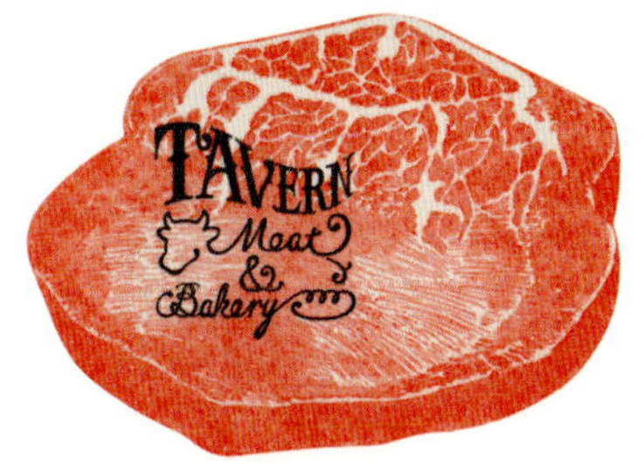

BAKERY CHEF
AZUSA MOGAMI

最上 梓

〒一五三-〇〇五一
東京都目黒区上目黒 一-五-七
代官山関ビル一階
1-5-7, Daikanyama Seki Bldg.1F,
Kamimeguro, Meguro TYO.153-0051 JP
T.03-6412-7644
U.www.conception-gp.com

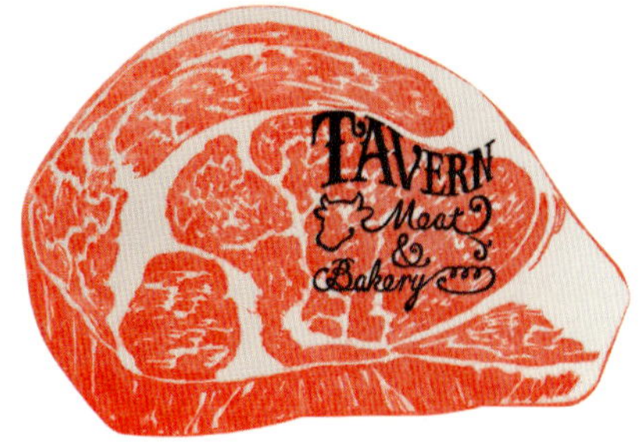

מרכז המבקרים של נמל חיפה

הוא בעל רעיון ייחודי המחבר בין העיר חיפה לנמל שלה. במרכז המבקרים תסיירו בין איזורים שונים שלכל אחד מהם התייחסות ייחודית אחרת לקשר בין העיר לנמל.

1 מרכז רב תרבותי
מאז since 1933

2 מרכז סחר וכלכלה
מאז since 1933

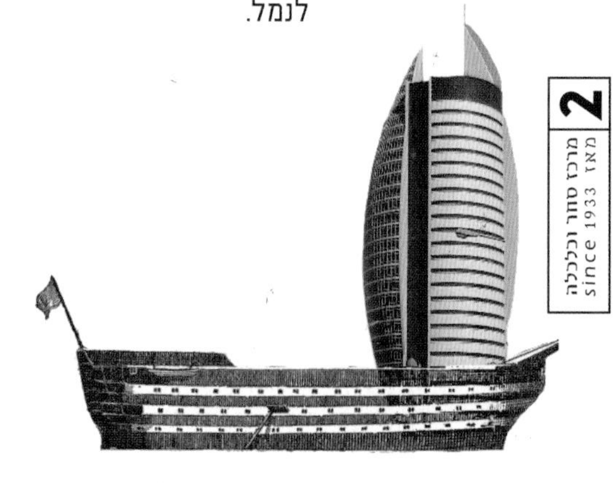

3 מרכז וותיק בעיר
מאז since 1933

4 מרכז חדש להשכלה
מאז since 1933

5 מרכז כח ותעשייה
מאז since 1933

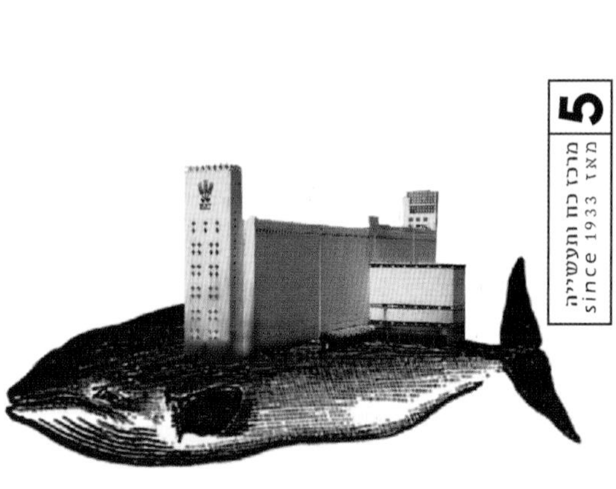

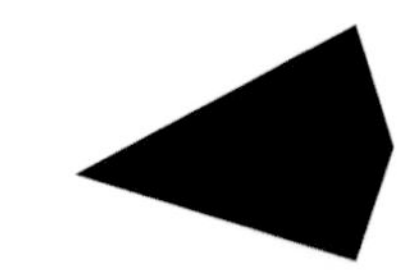

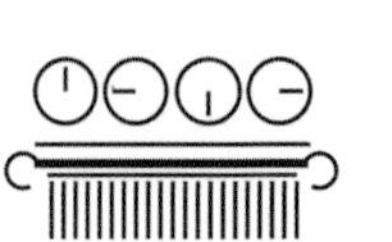

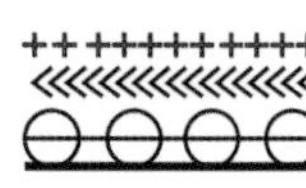

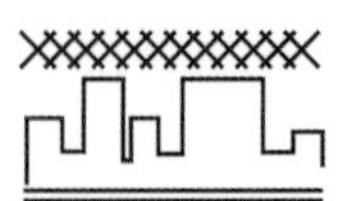

Haifa City Port

The Port of Haifa was established in 1929 by the British, who were looking to build their own port. It was established in the facade of the city. The port was built incorrectly in terms of urban architecture, and over the years has caused bad relations between the port and the Municipality of Haifa. Between the three cities in Israel that have a port, Haifa`s port is actually part of the city, and yet, the port is completely disconnected from the city. However, those who live nearby can sense that the port is an integral part of the city.

The purpose of the project is to show the integration of the port into the city; colliding harmoniously. The goal is to create a new world of images that would show us the harmony between the two worlds.

Client: Haifa City Port | Design: OR Shaaltiel, Arava Weinstein | Lecturer: Avigail Reiner (The NB School of Design) | Photography: Danielle Yashar

DI GUSTO
IN GUSTI
OSTERIA DELLA
VICTOR RUSSO

Victor Russo's Osteria

In Russo's Osteria taste sensations are experienced and shared. Accurate imagination through visual accuracy. The flavors of the traditional products are the main characters of the story, each with their own biography.

The Gorgonzola Picante, for example, a cow with snakelike traits, is the story of a local producer, told by Victor Russo and mastered by the dinner guests. The basis of the brand identity lies in the taste. A sense of ornamental symbolism has been built into the design. The representations, using 18th-century engravings, remind us of the fruit and vegetable portraits of the 16th century Italian painter Arcimboldo. These representations of taste are being used as key visuals for Russo's. The central logo affirms the representation. In the translation to the franchise formula the symbolism is consistent. In naming the individual trattorias, an endorsement structure is developed in which the nomenclature follows from the concept of "il traversare nei Gusti," for example: "Di Gusti in Gusti – Osteria della Victor Russo," "Stoccagio di Storia – Osteria della Victor Russo," and so on.

Client: Victor Russo | Design Agency: Total identity | Creative Direction: Felix Janssens | Design: Maarten Brandenburg | Copywriter: Felix Janssens

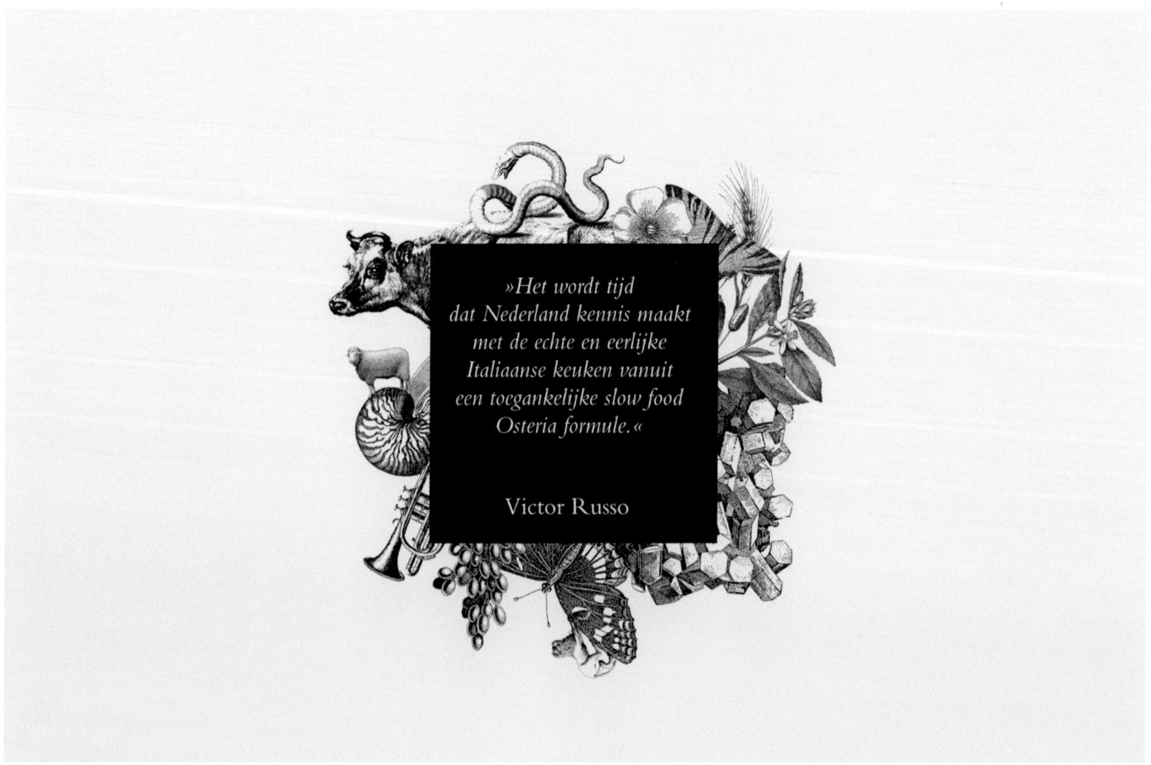

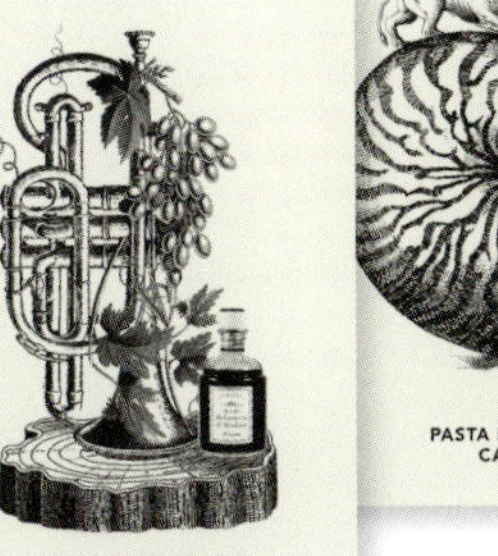

VICTOR
RUSSO'S
OSTERIA

'Donec et vehicula elit. Suspendisse nec orci libero, at pretium arcu. Lorem ipsum dolor sit amet, consectetur adip iscing elit. Vivamus id dui libero, vitae faucibus est. Donec et vehicula elit. Su spendisse nec orci libero, at pretium arc. Sed eget augue in mauris tempus vesti bulum nec vel mi. Lorem ipsum.

Victor Russo
Traverso di gusti!

Antonio Vivaldistraat 2-8
1083 HP Leiden
015 159 159 15
victorrusso.nl

#1.2011

Il Viaggio

VICTOR
RUSSO'S
OSTERIA
Antonio Vivaldistraat 2-8
1083 HP Leiden
victorrusso.nl

Lorem ipsum,

Dolor sit amet, consectetur adipiscing elit. Vivamus id dui libero, vitae faucibus est. Donec et vehicula elit. Suspendisse nec orci libero, at pretium arcu. Sed eget augue in mauris tempus vestibulum nec vel mi.Lorem ipsum dolor sit amet, consectetur adipiscing elit. Vivamus id dui libero, vitae faucibus est. Donec et vehicula elit. Suspendisse nec orci libero, at pretium arcu. Vivamus id dui libero, vitae faucibus est. Donec et vehicula elit. Suspendisse nec orci libero, at pretium arcu Donec et vehicula elit. Suspendisse nec orci libero, at pretium arcu.

Victor Russo

SAGRANTINO DI MONTEFALCO PAG.2

WINKEL

SLOW SALAMI CINTA SENESE

Donec et vehicula elit. Suspendisse nec orci libero, at pretium arcu. Sed eget augue in mauris tempus vestibulum.

TOSCAANSE PECORINO DI PIENZA

Donec et vehicula elit. Suspendisse nec orci libero, at pretium arcu. Sed eget augue in mauris tempus vestibulum.

BIOLOGISCHE TOPWIJNEN UIT SICILIË

Donec et vehicula elit. Suspendisse nec orci libero, at pretium arcu. Sed eget augue in mauris tempus vestibulum.

WORKSHOPS

TNT is onder de pannen pag.2

RECEPT

Pasta alla Florentina pag.4

RESTAURANT

Achtergronden bij de nieuwe kaart pag.3

Lorem ipsum dolor sit amet, consectetur adipiscing elit. Vivamus id dui libero, vitae faucibus est. Donec et vehicula elit. Suspendisse nec orci libero, at pretium arcu. Sed eget augue in mauris tempus vestibulum nec vel mi.

KOOKREIZENREIZEN

Zelf een uitje snijden in Umbrië pag.4

Lorem ipsum dolor sit amet, consectetur adipiscing elit. Vivamus id dui libero, vitae faucibus est. Donec et vehicula elit. Suspendisse nec orci libero, at pretium arcu. Sed eget augue in mauris tempus vestibulum nec vel mi.

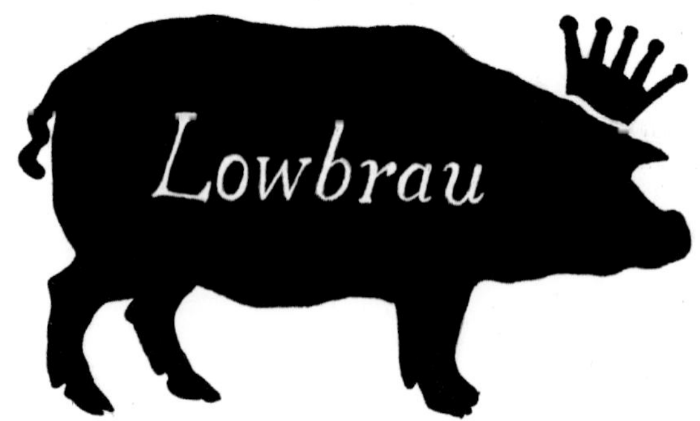

Lowbrau Beirhalle

In Germany, the beer hall is a communal gathering place where people can enjoy friends and family. Lowbrau is a modern spin on the traditional German Bierhalle. Portland, Oregon-based studio, Band, started collaborating with Michael Hargis in 2012 to help bring his concept to life. Located in the heart of Sacramento's midtown, Lowbrau features community tables, beers from the old country, and sausage to go with it. Band was involved in all aspects of the restaurant opening, from the initial concept development, and marketing, to overseeing all of the final collateral, interior design, and overall look and feel of the brand. Band aimed to help give Lowbrau some heart, and couldn't be more thrilled with how it all turned out.

Client: Lowbrau Beirhalle | Design Agency: Band | Photography: Chantel Elder

Trinken
HOUSE COCKTAILS
Belgian 75 $9.00
Munich Mule $9.00
Nice Pear $9.00
Nothing Rhymes $9.00
Cherry Cask $9.00
Hop Reviver $9.00
WINE
Railbridge $7.00
Railbridge $7.00
Chateau Saint Michelle $8.00
Chateau Saint Michelle $8.00
Freixenet $7.00
OTHER FARE
SALADS
SIDES
DESSERTS

Trinken
LOWBRAU
Essen

Madam Sixty Ate

There was a desire to create a strong brand based on the restaurant name "Madam Sixty Ate" in Hong Kong. Substance created the exploits of a mythical person that reflected the chef's vision, and the surprise pairing of ingredients.

Madam Sixty Ate is a mysterious adventurer and eclectic writer who delights us with her palate and imagination. Her worldview is modern with a twist, mirroring the style of food. Her surreal experiences, and astounding stories are reflected consistently through the brand using paintings, journal entries within menus, coasters, and ultimately throughout the cuisine. The journey from discovering a new restaurant, to the after dinner farewell, is a reflection of the journey Madam Sixty Ate embarked on.

Client: Madam Sixty Ate | Design Agency: Substance

STANLEY
The snapper swam alongside my raft as he paddled east. I lowered myself over the edge, and my body almost met the ocean as I reached for the snapper with my free hand. He blinked and squirmed in my grasp. After deciding to call it "Stanley", I laughed to wonder who would believe what I'd seen. I took a mental photograph of Stanley and tossed him back the fantastic deep

RIEDEL WINE GLASS

Kala

Kala is an official art merchandiser based on Resatio's collage artwork. Kala derived from Sanskrit language and means time, art, prosody, and small part of anything. Numerous meanings can be found in Kala, and those are our brand values: mysterious and surreal collage art are combined with beautifully rustic objects.

Client: Kala | Design: Resatio Adi Putra

S F · T F N
ANALYSIS

SF+TFN / Chain Reaction

This is a line of handcrafted merchandise for Teatro Fondamenta Nuove – the contemporary theater of Venezia complementary to the visual communication Studio Fludd designed for it.

3. CATALYSIS / Kit of Pins + 2. ANALYSIS / Set of Notebooks + 1. SYNTHESIS / Tote Bag are three illustrated items where various objects are involved in (fuzzy) chain reactions.

Client: Teatro Fondamenta Nuove | Design: Studio Fludd

Red By Wolves

Complete rebranding of up-and-coming shoe label, including a look book showcasing both the new season and classic Red By Wolves shoes. Building on the brand's established reputation for quality, tradition, and classic English styling, the ad campaign set the shoes amid an enchanting Lilliputian world created from vintage etchings. Two posters were loosely folded in the center spread.

Client: Red By Wolves | Design Agency: Foundry | Creative Direction: Matthew Schofield | Design: David Weller, Sunny Park | Photography: Doh Lee

RED BY WOLVES
LONDON

THIS IS OUR KINGDOM
www.redbywolves.com

RED BY WOLVES
LONDON

THIS IS OUR KINGDOM
www.redbywolves.com

Gemania

The value of a diamond lies far beyond it's worth, it captures feelings and emotions. Targeted at the middle class, this new jewelry brand identity designed by Tommy Li Design Workshop is based on the incredible tale of a treasure hunt near Pretoria, where the Star of Africa was found. Also included in the identity were elements of western culture, and a sense of middle class superiority. Although many new brands need time to build a reputation, Gemania jumped right into the market with great success and popularity.

Client: Gemania | Design Agency: Tommy Li Design Workshop Ltd. | Creative Direction: Tommy Li | Art Direction: Tami Leung | Design: Karen Chan | Illustration: Page Tsou

THE TALE OF
GEMANIA

THE TALE OF
GEMANIA

THE TALE OF
GEMANIA

GEMANIA

GEMANIA

B and C

Beto and Carlos are two friends that simply love eating. They aren't cooks, or world-renowned chefs, but their passion takes shape in delicious and laidback dishes that are created through simmering experimentation. The goal of this project was to create a brand that was both warm and inviting, with a style based on the magic that happens when a cook mixes ingredients together.

Client: B and C | Design Agency: Estudio Yeye | Creative Direction: Orlando Portillo | Art Direction: Orlando Portillo | Design: Gabriel Gutierrez | Copywriter: Estefania Araiza | Illustration: Orlando Portillo | Photography: Estudio Yeye

B & C

BEEF

WINE

LA CASA DEL BUEN PALADAR

A
FUEGO
LENTO

EL
TIEMPO
EXACTO

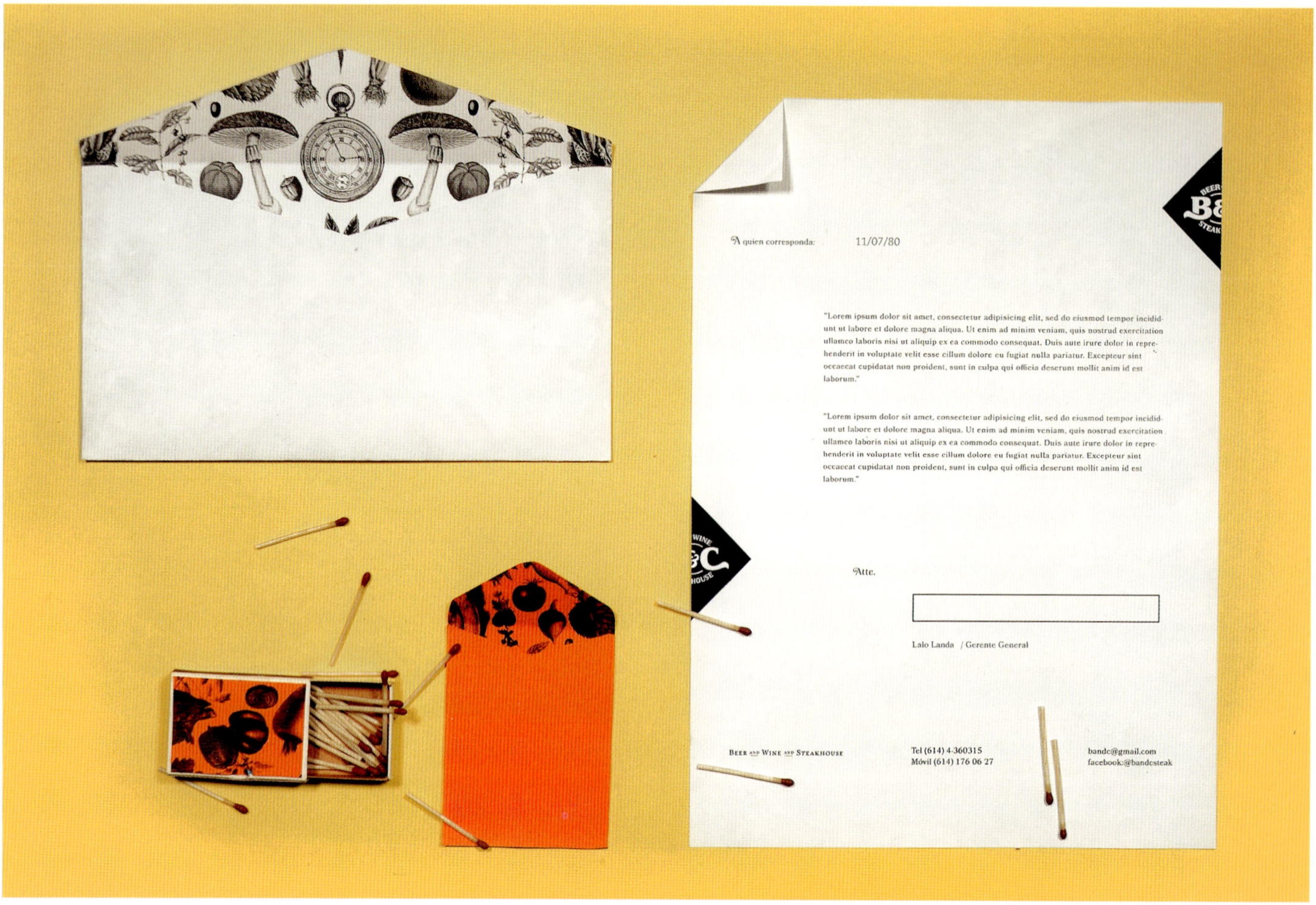

A quien corresponda: 11/07/80

"Lorem ipsum dolor sit amet, consectetur adipisicing elit, sed do eiusmod tempor incididunt ut labore et dolore magna aliqua. Ut enim ad minim veniam, quis nostrud exercitation ullamco laboris nisi ut aliquip ex ea commodo consequat. Duis aute irure dolor in reprehenderit in voluptate velit esse cillum dolore eu fugiat nulla pariatur. Excepteur sint occaecat cupidatat non proident, sunt in culpa qui officia deserunt mollit anim id est laborum."

"Lorem ipsum dolor sit amet, consectetur adipisicing elit, sed do eiusmod tempor incididunt ut labore et dolore magna aliqua. Ut enim ad minim veniam, quis nostrud exercitation ullamco laboris nisi ut aliquip ex ea commodo consequat. Duis aute irure dolor in reprehenderit in voluptate velit esse cillum dolore eu fugiat nulla pariatur. Excepteur sint occaecat cupidatat non proident, sunt in culpa qui officia deserunt mollit anim id est laborum."

Atte.

Lalo Landa / Gerente General

Beer and Wine and Steakhouse

Tel (614) 4-360315
Móvil (614) 176 06 27

bandc@gmail.com
facebook:@bandcsteak

Deliciosas
POSTRES
Tarta de manzana
Brownie americano
Copa de kiwi
Pie de aguacate
55

Refrescantes
BEBIDAS
Jamaica 20
Agua embotellada 15
Limonada 20
mineral o natural
Té verde o negro 20
refill
Café americano 18
Clamato 18
Refrescos 18
Línea Coca Cola
Pregunta por nuestra carta de vinos

Index

Index is a fashion brand based in Hong Kong, selling high quality clothing.

The key visuals are mainly generated by different kinds of raw materials, which are used to produce the clothing.

Client: Index | Design Agency: Fundamental | Design: Rayman

Marco Fadiga Bistrot

Creating a visual identity that plays with elegance and irony, as the bistro and the chef do. As for the website, it should have a simple structure as well as unique flavor. Complete branding project: logotype, letterhead and business cards, web site, menu, signage indoor and outdoor, posters, gadgets.

Client: Marco Fadiga Bistrot | Design Agency: Dina&Solomon by Manuel Dall'Olio and Mirit Wissotzky

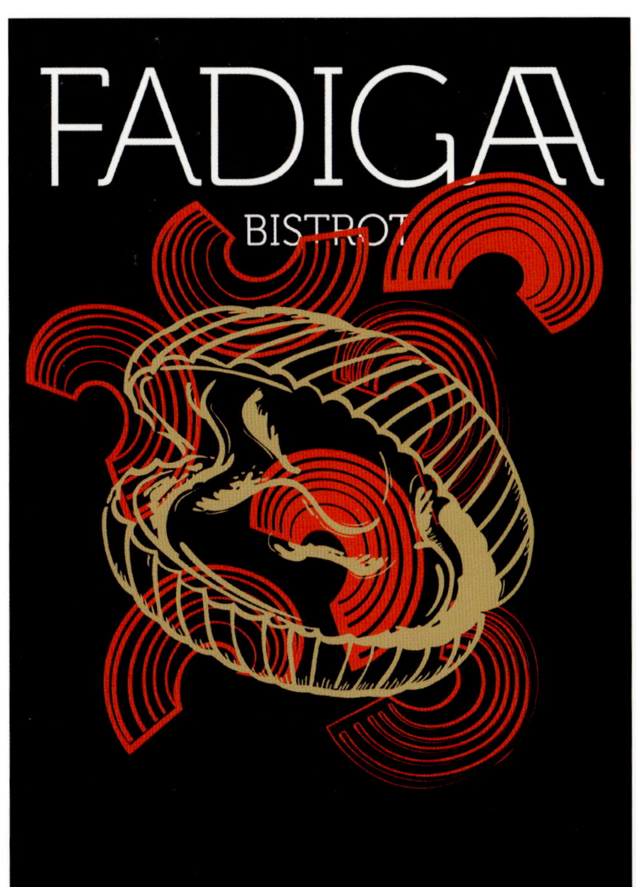
FADIGA
BISTROT

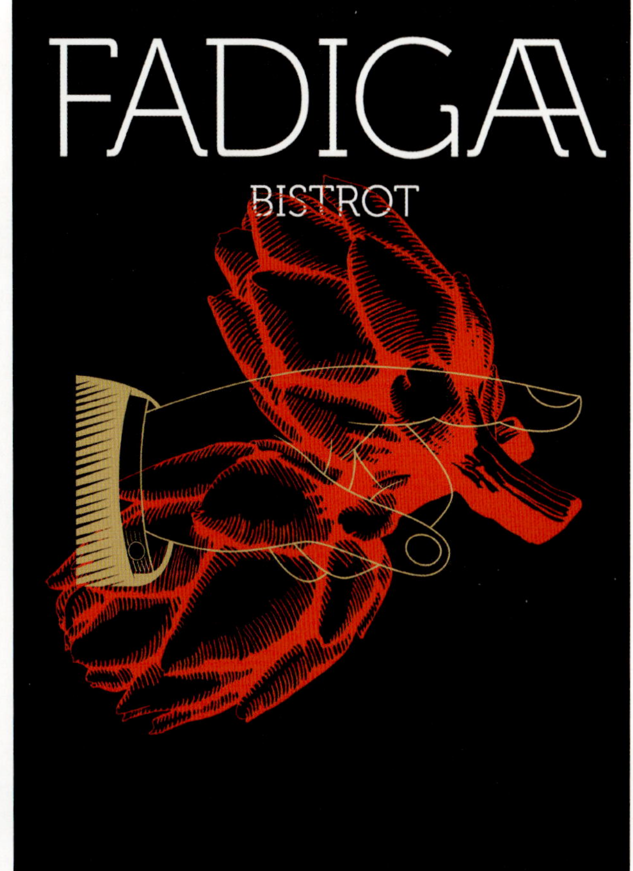
FADIGA
BISTROT

FADIGA
BISTROT
SPAGETTIS
BOLOGNAISE
SAUCE

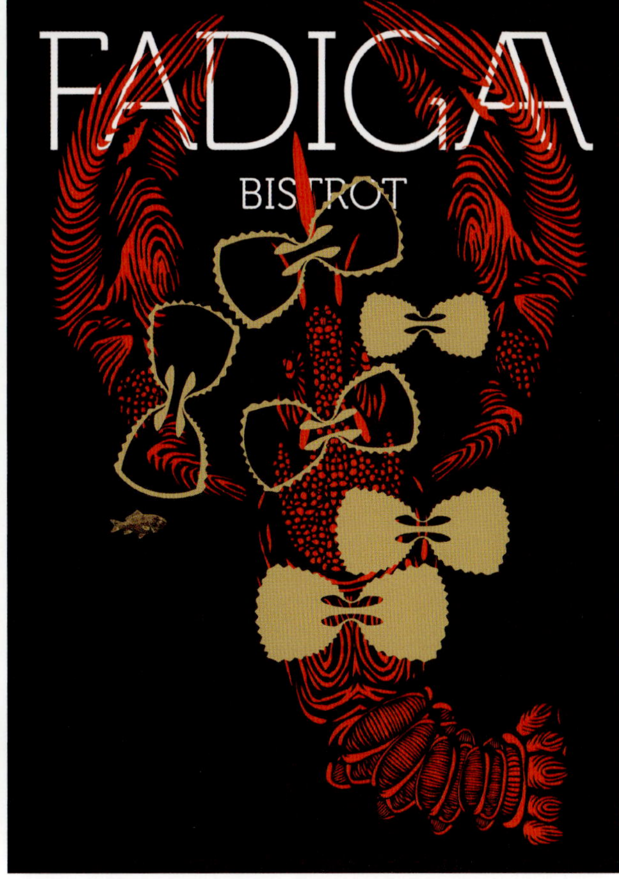
FADIGA
BISTROT

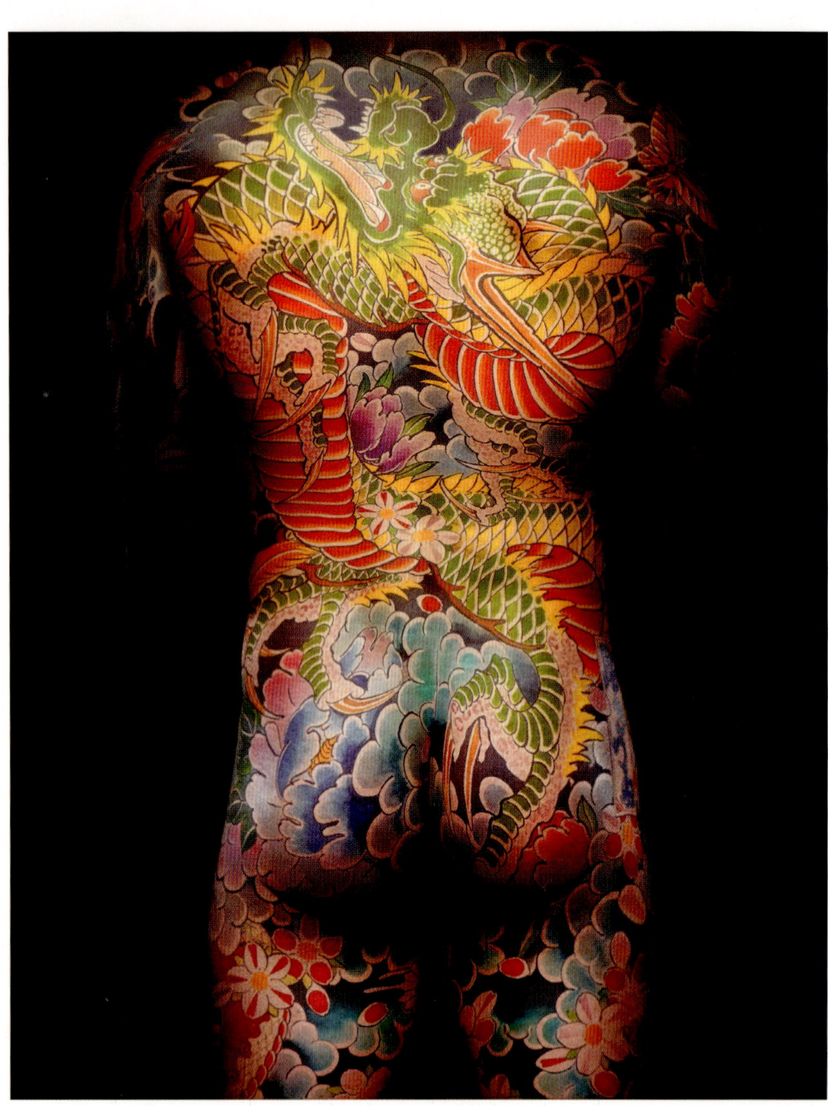

Miss Kō

An underground Asian fusion restaurant located in the heart of Paris' most prestigious arrondissement. Enter the world of Miss Kō, and find yourself transported to a busy Asian street. It's the future; a place where cultures collide, fantasy rules, and nothing is what it seems. It's Blade Runner – only happy. The logotype is simply 9 grains of rice; the staple of all Asian cuisine, and integral to the Asian way of life. Miss Kō is young, sexy, but eternally mysterious. She is a symbol of Asia, and the embodiment of its traditions and its strangeness. Her Yazuka tattoos reveal ties to an Asian underworld, and expose her rebellious nature. The Kō clan is set to grow as new restaurant openings in New York and elsewhere will each feature different tattooed characters. Miss Kō is a place to forget reality, indulge in fantasy, and become part of something unexplainable.

Client: Miss Kō | Design Agency: GBH | Creative Direction: Jason Gregory, Mark Bonner, Peter Hale | Art Direction: Peter Hale | Design: Bethan Jones | Tattoo: Alex Reinke | Photography: Uli Webber

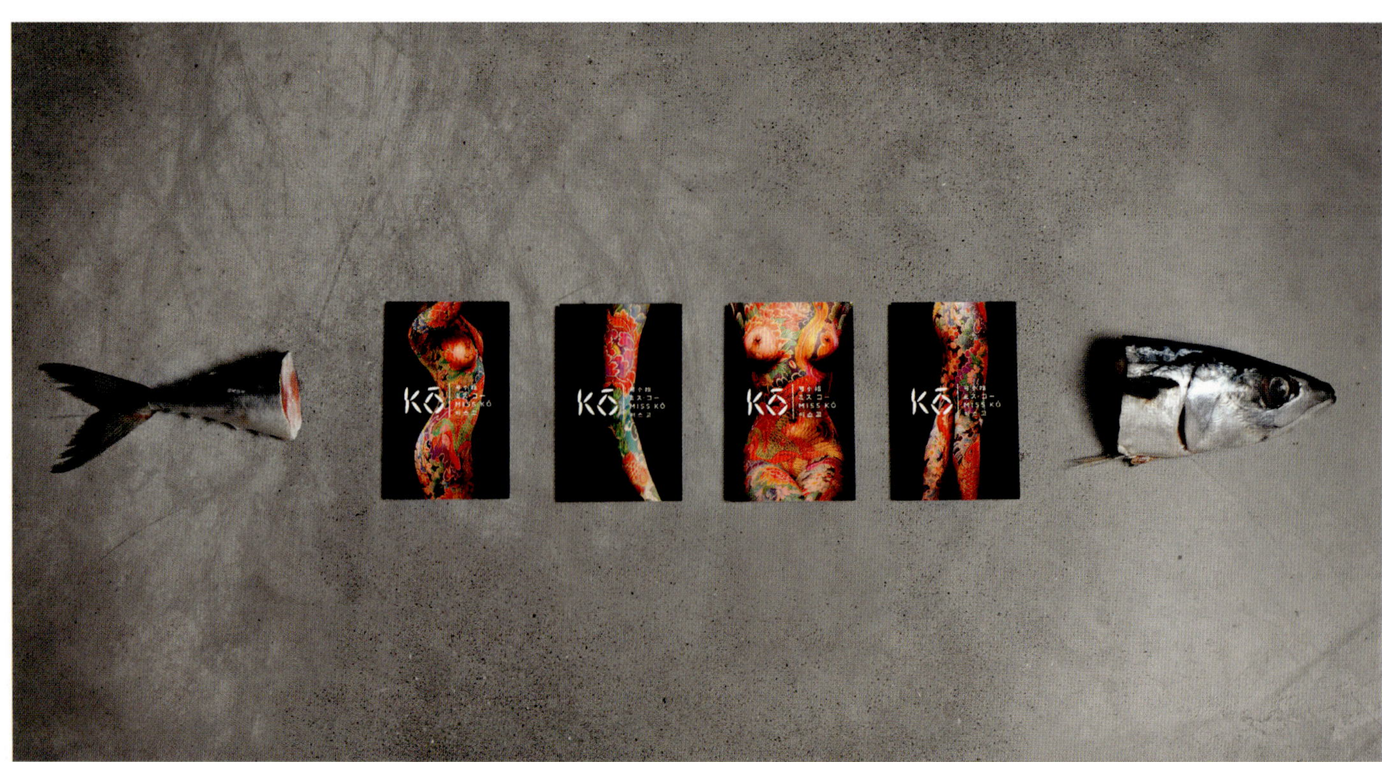

KŌ
MISS KŌ

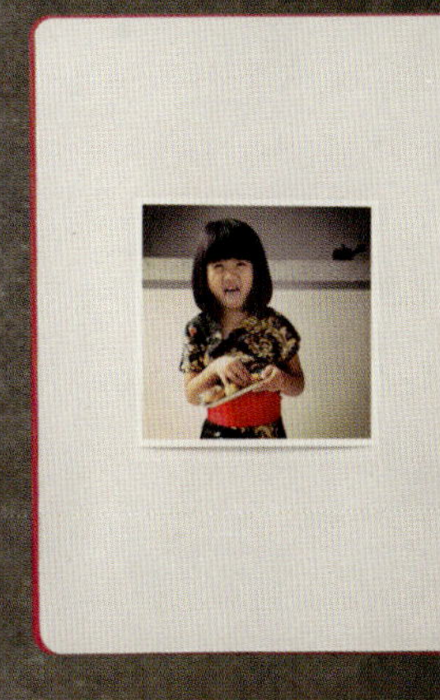

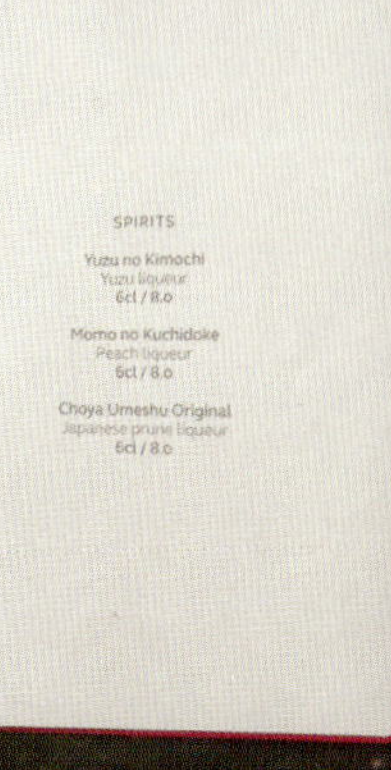
SPIRITS
Yuzu no Kimochi
Yuzu liqueur
6cl / 8.0
Momo no Kuchidoke
Peach liqueur
6cl / 8.0
Choya Umeshu Original
Japanese prune liqueur
6cl / 8.0

KŌ
MISS KŌ

KŌ
MISS KŌ

KŌ

MRS LI
Exotic yet traditional. An elegant fusion of genever, limoncello, Campari and lychee juice with the sweet, sour embrace of japanese umeshu plum liqueur. Finished with a rosebud iceburg.
€12.50

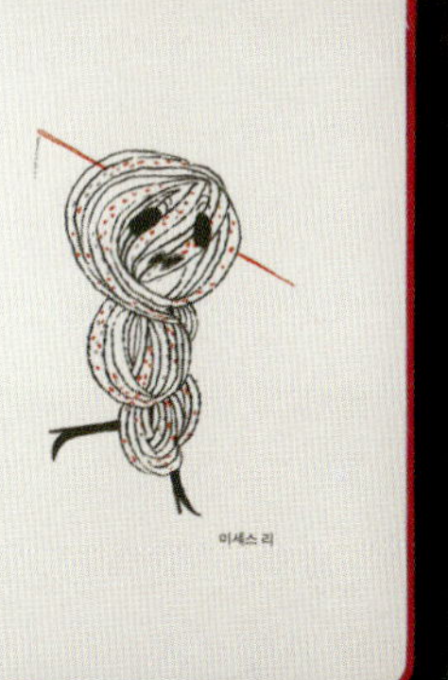

ICE CREAM
Chocolate-Nougat-Sesame
Vanilla-Ginger
Matcha Green Tea
SORBETS
Raspberry-Yuzu Coulis
Mango
Lychee-Grapefruit
One Flavour
4.0
Three Flavours
9.0

ADC Young Guns 8 Exhibition in Taiwan

Art Directors Club presented the Young Guns show to honor young designers under 30. 50 young designers were chosen to present in this exhibition that traveled the world. Kun Shan University in Taiwan, where the exhibition was held, commissioned Ken-tsai Lee to the develop the exhibition design. Lee said, when describing people who were outstanding from one another, he or she much have three heads and six arms. So, Lee asked illustrator Zhan Yu-Shu to create 50 monsters representing the 50 designers.

Client: Kun Shan University | Design Agency: Ken-tsai Lee/Taiwan TECH | Design: Ken-tsai Lee, Cheng, Chung-Yi | Illustration: Zhan, Yu-Shu

YG8-47
MARK WAR
Born 1981, London, UK
Mark Ward is a graphic artist based
elements inspired by Americana
with the everyday, encouraging the vie
A graduate of Central St. Martins, Mark wo
delivering strong concepts and bold
visuals to a range of clients. Projects include
NY ADC
YOUNGS

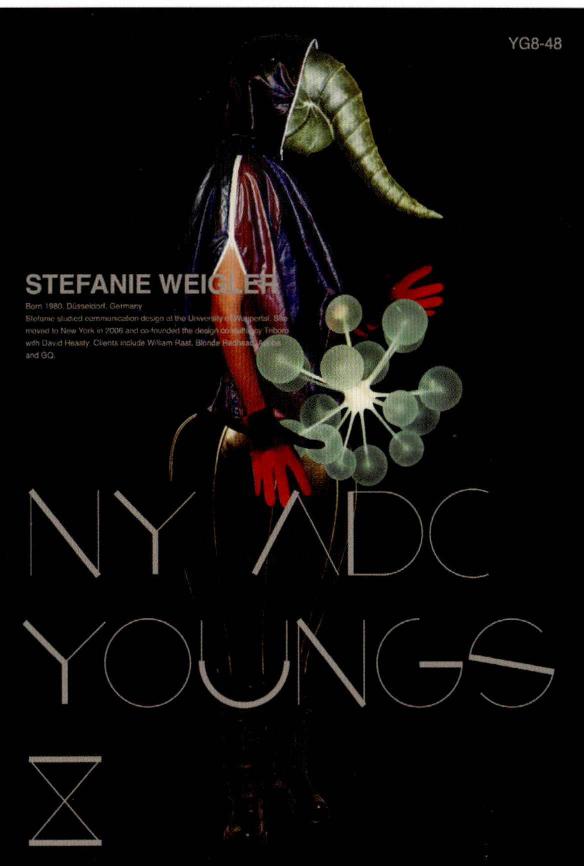
YG8-48
STEFANIE WEIGLER
Born 1980, Düsseldorf, Germany
Stefanie studied communication design at the University
moved to New York in 2006 and co-founded the design
with David Heasty. Clients include William Rast, Blonde
and GQ.
NY ADC
YOUNGS

YG8-49
IAN WHARTON
Born 1985, Preston, UK
I have always wanted to design and tell stories. In 2007 I graduated best-of-show from the University of Cumbria with a multi-award-winning short animated film. I have since been fortunate enough to work with some of the world's top brands and creative teams.
After working as Art Director at The Mill, I was appointed
Creative Director at 23 and led a global rebrand across London, NY and LA offices.
In 2010 I joined software publishing company Zolmo
Director and designed a top-grossing app for Jamie Oliver, later winning the Apple Design Award.
NY ADC
YOUNGS

YG8-50
JESEOK YI
Currently, Yale University (MFA)
republic of Korea
Formery, J.W.T New York, BBDO
FCB New York. Former clients
electronics Japan, KRAFT (Oreo)
Formery Advisor, The
dential Council for Future
& Vision
and Advertising
World Vision Seoul, The
Korea Green Foundation,
IAAF (World
Athletics Korea), Editor, Big Issue
NY ADC
YOUNGS

CROBIN
HELLO VON
ELSAE CHAVES &
TYLERLANG
ALWAYS WITH HONOR
SCOTT AMRON
ALEC BROWSTEIN
MIKEY BURTON
JONATHAN CALUGI
KELLIE CAMPBELL
FRANK CHIMERO
GEMMA CORRELL
JENNIFER DANIEL
MICHAEL FREIMUTH
CHRISTINE GIGNAC
JEREMY HALL
ERIC HU
GENKI ITO
NICOLE JACEK
E ROON KANG
STEPHEN KELLEHER
JEONG EUN
(ELLE) KIM
NY ADC
YOUNGS

MICAH LIDBERG
RIMANTAS LUKAVICIUS
TOMAS MANKOVSKY
JOE MARIANEK
SOPHIA MARTINECK
KENICHI MATSUMOTO
CARLES MURILLO
MARTIN NICOLAUSSON
LOTTA NIEMINEN
GARETH O'BRIEN
MITCHELL PAONE
STEVE PECK
GAVIN POTENZA
MADS JAKOB POULSEN
ALEX ROBBINS
NIKOLAY SAVELIEV
DAIHEI SHIBATA
KRIS SOWERSBY
NY ADC
YOUNGS

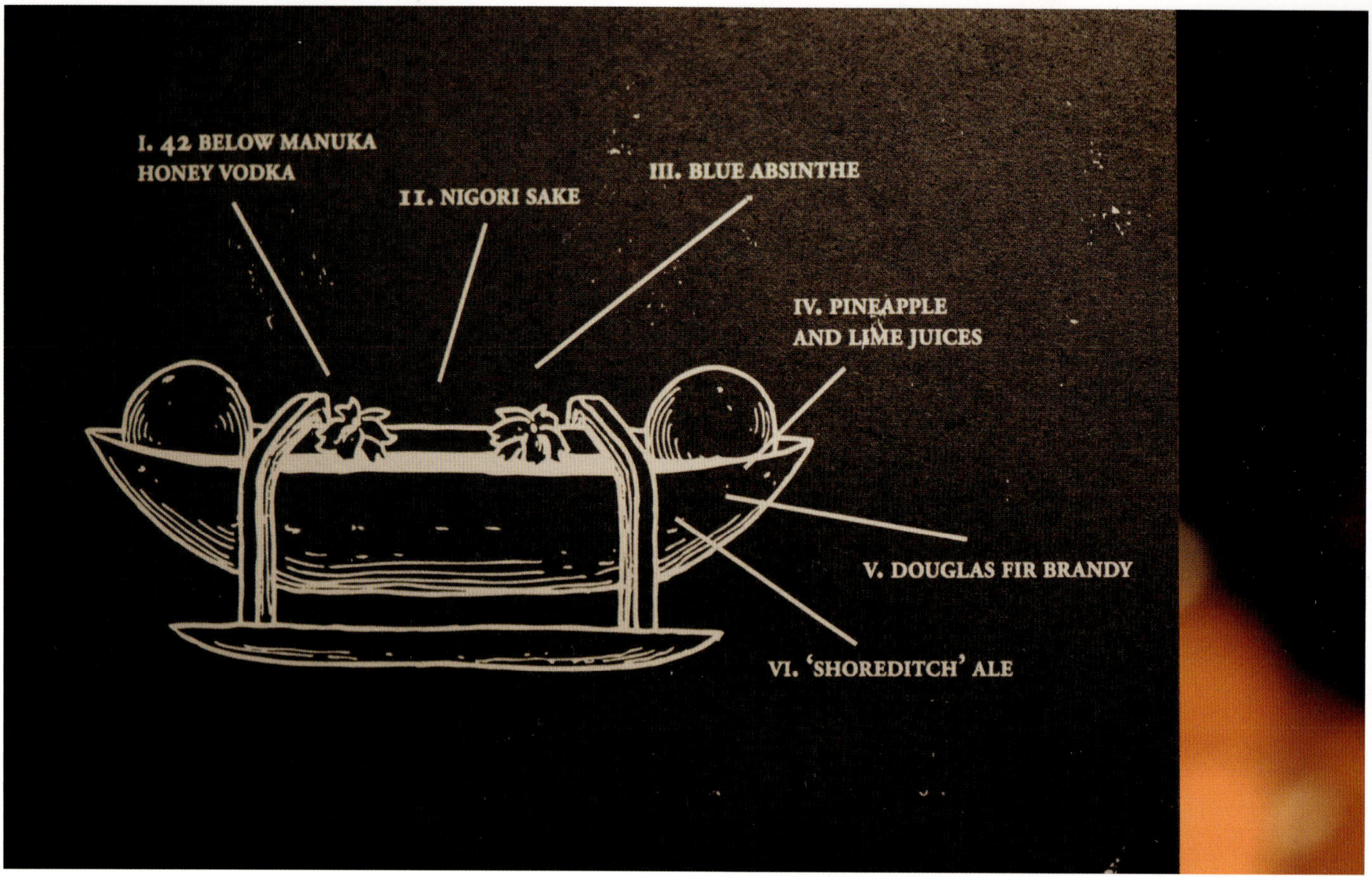

The Secret Bar

Speakeasies were places for illegal boozing that came to prominence during the Prohibition era in 1920's America. This nameless speakeasy-inspired bar has all the hallmarks of a trendy Singapore bar du jour.

There's a storefront location (The Library), hipster bartenders, an art-decor-meets-steam-punk interior, quirky presentation of cocktails – such as teacups brimming with gin – and a secret password to get in. Completing the quirky experience of this nameless brand, menus and business cards are made to look like secret manuals and recipes with eccentric scientific diagrams of the concoctions, named parts, and made-up Latin scientific names for the made-up mixing machines.

Client: JC Tapas | Design Agency: Foreign Policy Design Group | Creative Direction: Yah-Leng Yu | Art Direction: Yah-Leng Yu | Design: Willis Kingery, Bryan Lim | Photography: Jovian Lim

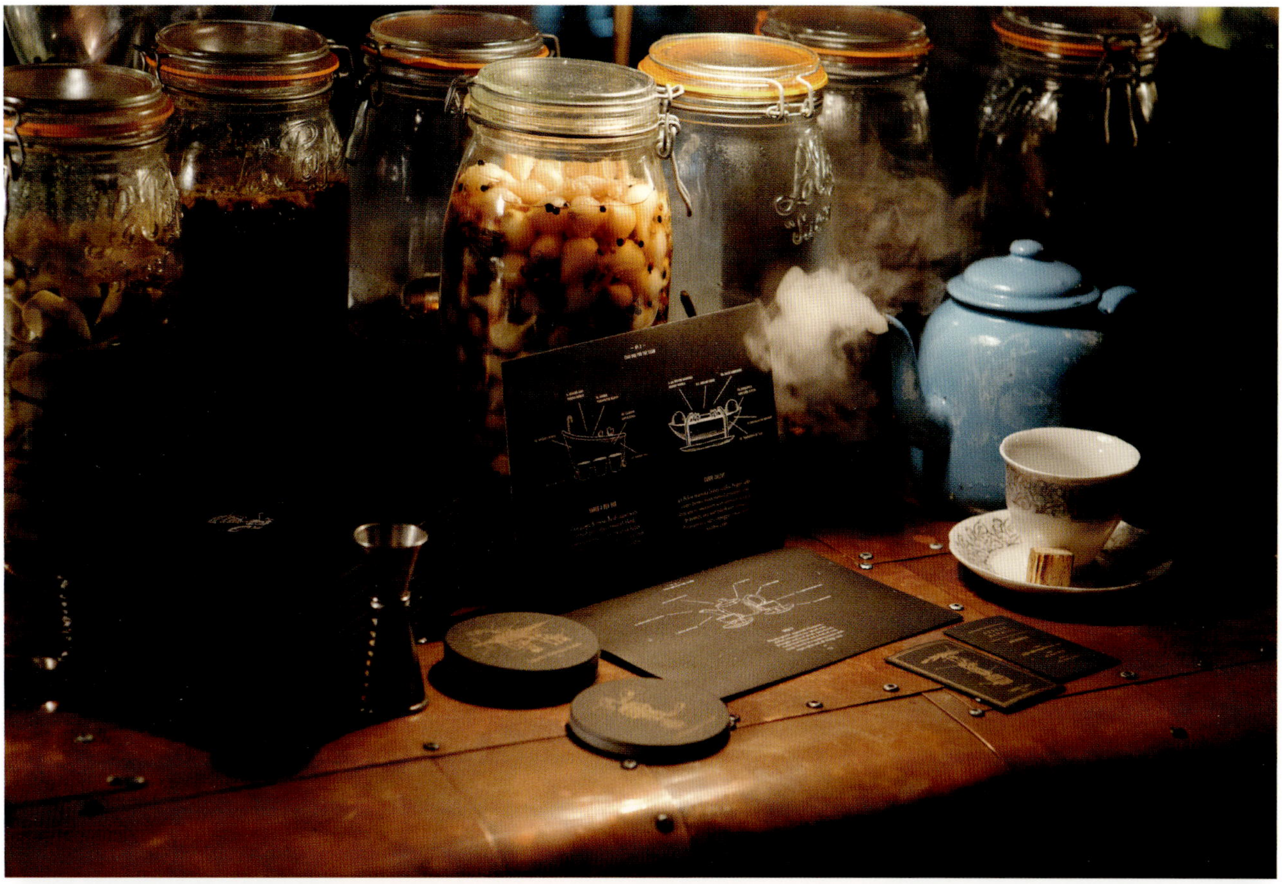

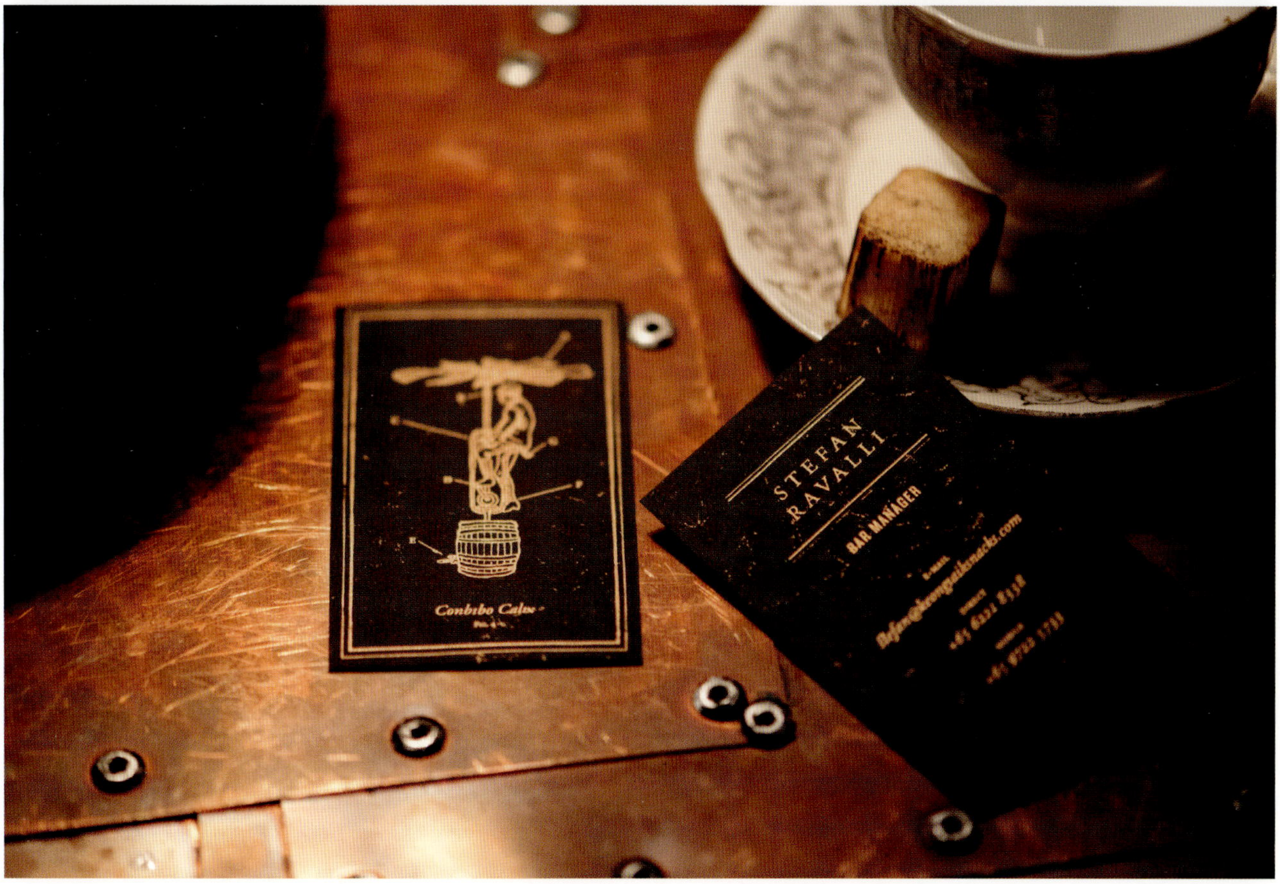
STEFAN
RAVALLI
BAR MANAGER

The National Bar & Dining Rooms

Love and War's branding for The National restaurant brings world-renown chef Geoffrey Zakarian's vision of "New York Grand Café" to life. The design is intended to be familiar and sophisticated, but with quirky touches and a dry wit befitting the New York City location and culture. A key motif in the brand design is a series of turn-of-the-century etchings reassembled into unique scenes and creations. These creations were incorporated into the design sparingly, and are often hidden for patrons to discover during their meal – tucked away on the inside cover of a matchbook, beneath a glass on a drink coaster, and so forth.

Client: Denihan Hospitality Group | Design Agency: Love and War | Creative Direction: Peter Tashjian, Eng San Kho | Art Direction: Katie Tully | Design: Minh Anh Vo, Victor Schuft, Steve Fine | Photography: Michael Guenther | Copywriter: Peter Tashjian

THE NTL.
THE NTL.
Bird Watching
THE NTL.
THE NTL.
THE NTL.
Strollophone

THE
NATIONAL
BAR & DINING ROOMS
STRIKE!

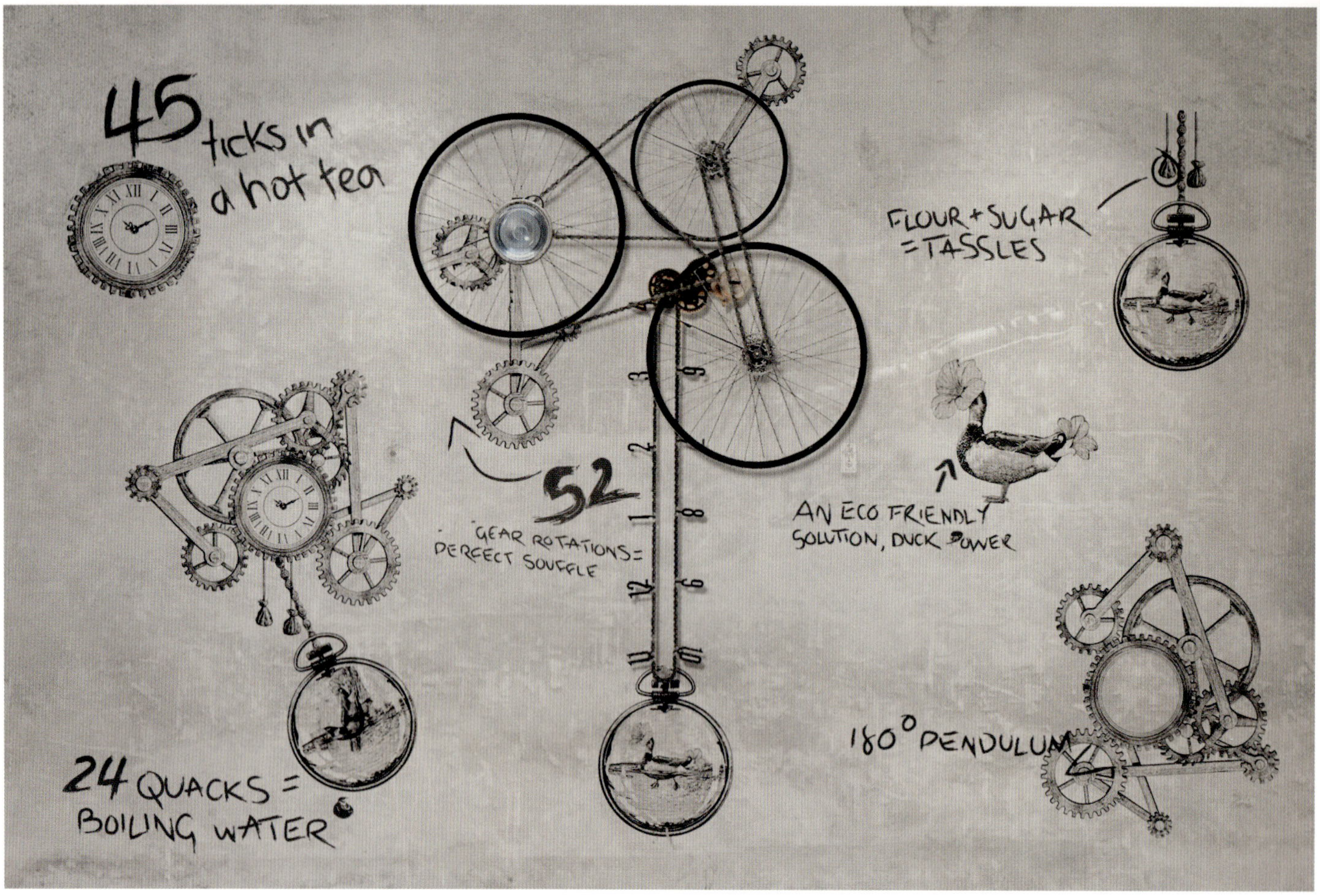

Sal Curioso

After the success of Madam Sixty Ate – a European restaurant founded by a whimsical chef of great imagination – Substance were appointed to brand a second restaurant with Spanish influences in the hub of Hong Kong's vibrant culinary scene. Sal Curioso is the name of Madam's Spanish ex-lover: an eccentric inventor and an uncommon genius.

Client: Elite Grace International Ltd | Design Agency: Substance

3 SHAKES OF PEPPER
+
2 SHAKES OF SALT
= PERFECT
GENTLE SLOPE
= NO BRUISING
HIGH POWER BLEND
3
PRECISION BLADES
2 SECONDS FLAT
LIGHT TOSS

Catalogue of failed MECHANISMS
MINIMALISM by Sal Curioso
A Rational Critique of Non-Mechanical Cooking
MAN'S SEARCH FOR THE MEANING OF SOUP
FORMULATING COOKING INSTRUMENTS

Montero

El Montero, is a restaurant located in Saltillo Coahuila, a city very close to Mexico's northern border. The project was developed and inspired by the colonial period, and with considered national patrimony. The development was executed with respect and care toward its elements. Anagrama's job as brand developers was to create a personality where we could glorify traditional kitchen values, and make the most of regional raw materials. For the interiors, we developed a project where antique elements could be combined with modern objects, allowing the space to communicate its gastronomical concept.

Client: El Montero | Design Agency: Anagrama

MONTERO
NUEVA COCINA RÚSTICA

INDEX

ACRE (P048-049)

Co-founded in 2011 by T Y Zheng and Jason Song, ACRE operates from the industrial heartlands of Singapore. They are an art collective of idea crafters. They believe the collaborative experience between clients and themselves ensures good design, clear communication, and holistic brand projection. Whether it's digital or print, ACRE are on good soil. They believe that untapped potential and limitless possibilities lie within the seed of every good idea.

www.acre.sg

AD&D (P192-193)

AD&D was established in 2011. Its founder graduated from Tohoku University of Art, and majored in sculpture. AD&D has received numerous accolades including: the NY TDC Judge's Choice Award (2011, 2013); One Show Award Merit Award (2011, 2012); China International Poster Biennial 2011 Finalist; 10th Francisco Mantecon International Advertising Poster Design Competition Finalist; Tokyo TDC Prize Nominee; The Brno Biennial 2012 Visitors' Award; Japan Typography Annual Best Work Award; D&AD 2012 IN BOOK; 91st NY ADC Silver; and the Jagda New Designer Award 2012.

www.ad-and-d.jp

ALONGLONGTIME (P050-051)

ALONGLONGTIME was founded in 2010, and is a Hong Kong-based multi-disciplinary design house. They specialize in brand identity, printed matter, and packaging for clients in corporate, leisure, retail, art, and culture.

ALONGLONGTIME aims to make design that is long lasting and meaningful; they believe design can be timeless and helpful to society. Every design they make goes through a long process and they work to answer each clients need on a project.

www.alonglongtime.me/

Anagrama (P052-053, 230-232)

Ideas exchanged generate constant inspiration, different points of view, and comprehension of their own views, all which complement their success. That is why Anagrama opens their doors with the best attitude, and continuously collaborate with press and education.

www.anagrama.com

Antonio Ladrillo (P163)

The work of Barcelona artist, Antonio Ladrillo, has been featured everywhere from intimate exhibitions to international galleries. He draws his influences from the chaotic lines of graffiti, contemporary art, and illustrators.

Antonio's experience creating paintings, commercial media, graffiti, and illustrations fuels his production of exuberant expressions that have the power to make just about anyone smile.

www.antonioladrillo.com

Arava Weinstein (P194-195)

Arava Weinstein is a graphic design student at Wizo Haifa Academy of Design and Education B. Ed. And she lives in Haifa, Israel.

www.behance.net/aravuva

Arthur Foliard (P166-167)

Arthur Foliard is a young Frenchman, who recently graduated with a degree in visual communication studies. He worked for 7 months at Landor Associates in San Francisco, and is currently working at Pentagram in London. He has been practicing design for just 3 years, and hopes to acquire more experience. For him, the most exciting thing about this job is the feeling of learning new things every day.

www.arthurfoliard.com

Band (P198-199)

Band is a studio based in Southeast Portland. Together, they are thinkers, creators, artists, graphic designers, illustrators, printmakers, woodworkers, welders, and more. They like to collaborate with good people on meaningful, worthwhile projects. They came together out of a love for the same 4 chords of fast music. Like the tones of those trusty chords, they strive to make a resonant sound in the world that is honest, pure, and all their own.

madebyband.com

Bec Kilpatrick (P170-171, 182-183)

Bec Kilpatrick is an artist based in Sydney, Australia. Drawing is central to Bec's practice from concept development through to final rendering. Her illustrations are highly detailed and can be seen across a wide range of applications from branding to product design. She is inspired by patterns in nature, and abstract forms creating unique and interesting compositions.

www.beckilpatrick.com

BLOW (P168-169)

BLOW is a Hong Kong-based design studio founded by Ken Lo in 2010. Specialized in branding, identities, packaging, environmental graphics, print, publications, and website design, they provide clients with mind-blowing designs that are simple, but bold in their approach. They believe that an effective design is not simply a cosmetic change to an appearance. It should be an overall brand platform derived from a unique brand positioning, clear definition of the target audience, and an understanding of the market and competitive environment. Eventually, it can help clients analyze the real problems of their business, and tackle them with the right strategy.

www.blow.hk

Bravo Company (P163)

Bravo Company is a creatively led, independent design studio based in Singapore. They work with a variety of individuals and organizations to deliver considered and engaging design. They specialize in identity and brand development, printed communications, and art direction.

www.bravo-company.info

Bruketa&Žinić OM (P078-079)

Bruketa&Žinić OM is a group of marketing communications agencies consisting of advertising agencies Bruketa&Žinić OM Zagreb (Croatia), Bruketa&Žinić OM Vienna (Austria), Popular Bruketa&Žinić OM Beograd (Serbia), Bruketa&Žinić OM Baku (Azerbaijan), brand consultancy Brandoctor, and digital agency Brlog and Brigada – a studio for designing efficient retail, exhibition and office spaces, product design and architecture.

The agency was founded by Davor Bruketa and Nikola Žinić in 1995. The group numbers some 80 creatives and experts in brand strategy, packaging design, graphic, spatial, and product design, strategic planning and every kind of on and off line marketing communication. The agency has launched its own brand of clothing Brokula&Ž (Broccoli&Ž) made of specially developed fabric from organically grown raw materials.

bruketa-zinic.com

Bureau FFabienne (P086-087)

FFabienne Bureau is an agency for commercial art and design. They work in the areas of art direction, graphic design, illustration, and event design.

www.ffabienne.com

C Plus C Workshop (P112-113)

C Plus C Workshop combines creativity and communication. Their workshop focuses on the interaction between design and visual communication.

They encompass a broad scope of areas from graphic design, advertising and branding, corporate communication, and identity. Although the three designers pursue their developments in different fields, they discovered that they have the same goal. Therefore, they formed C plus C Workshop to allow them to create their common creations, and search a base for their goal.

www.cplusc-workshop.com

Caroline Morris (P132-133)

Caroline Morris was born and raised in Nashville, Tennessee. She is deeply influenced by her roots in the south, and finds inspiration from the culture that surrounds her. Food, vintage type, paper, music, textiles, architecture, travel, and literature all contribute to her design process.

carolinemmorris.com

Codefrisko (P012-013)

Codefrisko is a graphic design and art direction studio specializing in culture, fashion, architecture, design, and the food industry.

www.codefrisko.be

Comuniza (P036-037)

Comuniza is communication strategy. They believe in the value of brands and the power of communication. They research, analyze, consult, are action-oriented, and connect between brands, and their content.

They define the elements necessary to include every corporate message, identify the target audience and discover their needs and motivations. They conduct proper planning of medium and message; they establish the relational and experiential mechanisms, and they set a timetable and deliver.

www.comuniza.com

Daria Karpenko (P124-125)

Daria Karpenko is a graphic designer and illustrator from Russia. She graduated from British Higher School of Art and Design in Moscow. She loves creating things – whether it's illustration or identity, or anything else – she concentrates on ideas. She also loves to work with her hands instead of a computer – it means that she uses a variety of printmaking techniques, paper craft, embroidery, and she likes to choose the paper for printouts very carefully. All these things help her to dip in her work, to enjoy the process, and fill the outcome with her energy and inspiration.

cargocollective.com/dashakarpenko

Design Studio of Both (P108-109)

Design Studio of Both is a young graphic design studio, founded by Àxel and Alba Durana and is located in Barcelona. They specialize in identity, editorial, and web design. Taking great interest in typography, and the proper organization of information, they are able to facilitate an understood message.

designstudioofboth.com

Designers Anonymous (P102-103)

This team is behind a broad mix of clients from a variety of sectors, each with individual objectives and audiences. They all share a common goal – to communicate in the most compelling, informative, and effective way that's true to their brand.

They help their clients reach their objectives and audiences with award-winning ideas, executed appropriately – across print, packaging, digital, animation, and video.

www.designers-anonymous.com

DESIGNER+ARTIST (P190-191)

The character "Ho"(和) is simple and balanced, and the visual sharpness and clean-cut feel of its design gives abundant willpower to simplicity. The studio hopes their heartfelt design will inspire every austere soul to examine work more closely.

"Ho" is to commemorate the cooperative teamwork between designer and artist, turning design into creation, and turning art into design planning. When the smaller "Ho" becomes the larger "Hokou"(禾口), it is an extension of overall abilities. When designers and artists gradually expand their ranks, they increase the will for "+." This cooperation is the professional integration between the different fields of art and design. You need to find the right people to do the right job. Using the vision of mutual support and division of labor, they provide professional service teams for visual designs, such as flat design, website design, and overall integrated planning for interdisciplinary art.

dxa.tw

Dry Design (P114-115)

Dry Design was founded in 2010 by collaboration between Carolina Cloos and Francesca Mezzetti. It's a young, but not inexperienced reality. They analyze customer needs and find the best solution to combine imagination and rationality. Graphic visual clarity and consistency is our approach to each new project. Their work ranges from print to web, and they take care of communication entirely.

www.dry-design.it

End of Work (P184-185)

End of Work is a Sydney-based branding and design consultancy specializing in intelligent, strategically sharp design solutions. It's their belief that brilliant ideas are the lifeblood of successful businesses. As a result, they are in constant pursuit of solutions that distinguish clients' brands in the marketplace, enhance value, and change the way people think.

For every idea they generate, they find an elegant and meaningful form of delivery. These range from the printed page, to digital and physical environments, but every one has a common thread – their trademark obsession with beautifully crafted visual communication. End of Work has created acclaimed work for a diverse range of Australian and international clients.

www.endofwork.com.au

Estudio m Barcelona (P084-085)

After many years working each in other disciplines, in late 2006, Estudio m Barcelona decided to get together to test a new formula. They are convinced that if you think about as a collective from the start, it becomes a consistent thing, one discipline building on the other. They eat breakfast every day together and share a table. Imagine what an architect can see in a packaging, or a graphic designer in a wall. If the interiors are done by one person, and the graphic design by another, surely everyone is working in a different direction. It may not disturb (at best), but it is unlikely they will complement, let alone work together to make a brand "talk" in all its manifestations with a single, coherent voice. They strive to have an emotional link with the customer, and this is not achieved simply by decorating a space with a logo or corporate colors, they believe it requires a much more subtle and intangible language. They like to say things, be it on paper, in a space, or through an object. Any medium is capable of telling a story. They believe more in practice than in theory. Until they see it, it is not worth much. Good design requires intuition and common sense. It sounds so obvious, and yet it is so difficult. Besides the projects that bring together the two disciplines, each continue working in their field.

www.m-m.es

estudio mllongo (P096-097, 100-101)

Estudio mLlongo is a Spanish creative studio formed by professionals from different fields of design and communication. This multidisciplinary character allows them to develop projects in several areas such as art direction, graphic design and communication, product design, stand design, interiors, and multimedia.

mllongo.com

Estudio Yeye (P210-213)

Since 2010, Estudio Yeye has been offering graphic design and illustration services for many formats. They also provide interior design and innovative branding and marketing solutions. Their objective is simple: to provide clients with a high quality result that is relevant, innovative, and ultimately impulses the growth of their client's business.

www.estudioyeye.com

Eszter Laki (P186-189)

Eszter Laki was born in Budapest, Hungary in 1983, and graduated from the Printmaking Program at the University of Fine Arts, Budapest in 2007. After this, she studied Typography at the University of Applied Arts. Since then, she has focused on her own art and design projects, and has been working as a freelancer graphic designer in the Flatlab co-working studio.

www.behance.net/lakieszti

Fabio Ongarato Design (P026-027)

Design continues to play a more important role in contemporary discourse because it deals with the way we feel. For all of us, design must be an experience regardless of medium; whether it is print, environmental graphics, or identity creation, the outcome must stand out and truly connect.

Designers in Fabio Ongarato Design are compelled by the view that design is a cultural imperative, and so see it as his or her personal responsibility to create a heightened experience that engages emotionally and intellectually. This view leads to ideas that find form beyond one dimensional expressions, with the designers owning and guiding the multilayered design process; working closely with clients to understand their marketplace and their perspective in order to determine a unique voice that is our client's – not our own; a unique voice that reflects an enduring, differentiated point of view. Their work is informed through strategically-driven thinking and research that it is distinctive and goes beyond the expected; ensuring the outcomes surprise, delight, reassure, and engage themselves. Such feelings are the product of their broad ranging craft, and the essence of the work detailed in this website.

www.fabioongaratodesign.com.au

FLOZ (P062-063)

FLOZ is an art direction and graphic design studio founded in 2010 in Paris, by Kathia Saul, Rémi Andron and Thiébaud Chotin. Their practice combines sophistication, precision, and experimentation. They help their clients design and develop their projects through: art direction (global art project management, direction of photo shoots, image consulting), visual identity (logo, branding, graphic design, and signage), editorial design/print (catalog, brochure, press, poster, and printed medias), and digital design (website, web communication).

Attentive to the overall project design, they build graphic and typographic dimension, and think on the choice of materials and manufacturing methods. They are tuned in and curious about the originality of each project, and they regularly work in collaboration with fashion, design, movie and visual arts professionals. FLOZ loves good looking books, photography, the smell of paper, and unexpected contrasts.

www.floz-studio.com

Foreign Policy Design Group (P146-147, 224-225)

Foreign Policy Design Group is a team of idea makers and storytellers who help clients and brands realize and evolve their brands with creative and strategic deployment of traditional terrestrial channels and digital media channels. Helmed by Creative Directors Yah-Leng Yu and Arthur Chin, the group works on a smorgasbord of projects ranging from creative/art direction and design, branding, brand strategy, digital strategy, strategic research, and marketing campaign services for luxury fashion and lifestyle brands, fast-moving consumer goods brands, arts and cultural institutions, as well as think tank consultancies.

foreignpolicydesign.com

Foundry (P206-207)

Foundry is an independent design and branding agency based in East London. They work across a range of disciplines including print and digital design, photography, illustration, copywriting, way finding, and exhibition graphics.

The studio practice is shaped by a diverse skill set and inter-disciplinary approach. A deliberately small and personalized studio, they work with multinational companies, independent brands, and individuals.

www.foundrystudio.com

Fundamental (P214-215, 110-111)

Fundamental is a Hong Kong-based creative studio. They believe that substantial communication is the key to creating and providing the best designs and solutions for their clients.

fundamental-studio.com

GBH (P218-219)

GBH is a London-based design and advertising agency founded in 1999 by Jason Gregory, Mark Bonner and Peter Hale. Since its inception, GBH has consistently been ranked amongst the top design agencies worldwide.

www.gregorybonnerhale.com

HaritaMetod (P014-015)

Ervin Esen is an Istanbul-based designer. After earning his BA from Marmara University in Turkey, and working at various ad agencies, he moved to London. There he studied Communication Design in Kingston University where he got his MA, and then worked alongside influential designer Vaughan Oliver designing CD and vinyl covers for bands like Cocteau Twins, Modern English, and This Mortal Coil. After a yearlong experience as a senior designer at Draught Associates, he moved back to Turkey to set up his own design studio, HaritaMetod.
His work has been published both nationally and internationally, and HaritaMetod continues to work with many clients locally and globally.

www.ervinesen.com / haritametod.com

Jean Jullien (P080-081)

Jean Jullien is a French graphic designer living and working in London. He comes from Nantes and earned a graphic design degree in Quimper before landing to London. He graduated from Central Saint Martins in 2008, and from the Royal College of Art in 2010. He works closely with the musician Niwouinwouin. His practice ranges from illustration to photography, video, costumes, installations, books, posters, and clothing to create a coherent, yet eclectic body of work.

www.jeanjullien.com

Johan Hjerpe (P016-019)

Johan Hjerpe is a designer based in Stockholm, Sweden. For the past decade Johan has been designing graphics, spaces, and strategic frameworks for a vast array of contexts. From working with Sweden as a nation brand, to doing commissions for magazines, artists, and fashion designers, stopping over in finance, electronics, white goods, performing arts, and more. Over the years his work has gained a focus on the sociocultural aspects of people interacting. Design becomes a tool, prop, or interface for situations where mutual value-in-context emerges.

www.johanhjerpe.com

Just a Kiss (P106-107)

Jak (for Just a Kiss) is a Parisian branding and advertising agency created in 2007 by Arnaud Pigounides. As designer associate in Absolution, he has won many awards, including the Wallpaper Design Award 2010.

www.justakiss.fr

Kathy Wu (P090-091)

Kathy Wu is a graphic design student currently pursuing a BFA at Rhode Island School of Design, class of 2015. Her background in illustration and her love of drawing determine that she will never stop savoring the handmade mark. She believes in design that is fun-spirited, atypical, and memorable and believes in design that can be taken apart and enjoyed with your hands. "Chocolee" is her first independent branding project, and that space in the Venn diagram where all of her passions – illustration, graphic design, and pattern design – merge in the spirit of playful packaging.

behance.net/kathywu

Ken-tsai Lee Image Design Company (P220-223)

Ken-tsai Lee was born in Taipei, currently living in New York, and established Ken-tsai Lee Design Studio since 1996. Since 2002, he has moved to New York to continue his career. His partner Chou Yao-Fong who keeps the studio still working in Taipei. After Came to New York, Lee's tried different media and cooperated with other fields of professionals, such as photographer, animator to explored new methods of design. Ever since the establishment of Lee's own studio, he has won numerous design awards and participated many design exhibitions worldwide, such as D&AD Awards, Communication Arts Design Annual Awards, New York Type Director Club Annual Awards, One Shoe Design Award, Red-Dot Awards Communication Design, Tokyo Type Directors Club Annual Awards and etc.

www.behance.net/kentsailee

Kinetic Design and Advertising (P088-089)

Kinetic is a creative agency based in Singapore.

www.kinetic.com.sg

Kokoro & Moi (P070-071)

Kokoro & Moi, established in 2001, is a full-service creative agency transforming brands with bold ideas, and progressive concepts. Their focus is on strategy, identity, and design. They are always asking questions, challenging norms, and piecing together new worlds to solve tasks in unique ways. It's a playground out there, so they just play with what they can with no preconceptions. In a world overloaded with messages, they use the power of design to help their clients stand out.

They create authentic and innovative strategies, craft imaginative solutions and make an impact in the required media – from print and digital, to products and environments. There's always a way. However, they believe each case is unique and collaborative. They have worked alongside a broad and international range of commercial players, from multinationals, to start-ups as well as a variety of cultural and public institutions.

This is how they intend to continue – setting the standard, and then continuing to evolve it.

www.kokoromoi.com

La Tortillería (P060-061)

Originally founded in an old tortilla factory building, La Tortillería is a creative company with a passion for images and words, with the exceptional ability of turning them into an exquisite reflection of an idea. They create, brand, design, publish, and advertise – blending creativity and functionality to grant each project a unique personality. They start out with the end picture in their mind, and are creative problem solvers who make things happen come hell or high water.

www.latortilleria.com

Leo Karhunen (P120-121)

Leo Karhunen has been working in the field of graphic design for 10 years. Whether in design, concepts or illustrations, he aims to inspire as well as inform. He works for both cultural and commercial clients, including Heineken, Nike, Adidas, Artek, and Iittala.

leokarhunen.com

Les Bons Faiseurs (P126-127)

Les Bons Faiseurs is a versatile graphic design agency based in Paris. In love with great ideas and intelligent design, Les Bons Faiseurs work for a variety of brands and institutions as well as on identities, packaging, and diverse communication projects.

www.lesbonsfaiseurs.com

Liow Heng Chun (P030-031)

Liow Heng Chun is a compulsive dreamer, who survives on imagination, and dreams big. An active learner, he prides himself on the insatiable appetite for thinking incorrectly, and making interesting mistakes. A craftsman of betterment, he makes things more awesome and worthwhile for the people who use or encounter them, with soul and love. A typography enthusiast, he sees each typeface as friends who have distinctive personality. He is a resolute believer in the power of beauty, and how it is capable of making huge changes or differences to the world.

www.behance.net/anotherphilip

Livingroom Communication, UAE (P066-067)

A place partners and brands call home. Conversations have evolved. They don't just talk anymore they share everything, everywhere. They share points of views. They share moments. They share feelings. They share the day. And they share a bit of ourselves for one reason, to stay connected.

www.me-livingroom.com

Love and War (P226-227)

When they were on the client side, Love and War is the agency they wanted to hire, but couldn't find. It is the company they wanted to work for, but couldn't unearth. Instead of departmental silos, they wanted a single "go to" team that could attack problems, develop creative solutions, and execute across print, web, and broadcast media. They wanted to work with people who had an intuitive grasp of brand strategy, and a knack for breakthrough creative. They wanted a streamlined structure, and a flexible process. They wanted to work with people who would roll up their sleeves and get it done. They couldn't find the agency they wanted. So they created it.

www.loveandwar.com

Luís Mendonça (P176-177)

Luís Mendonça has been highlighted in Portugal for his intense and prolific activity as illustrator, designer, and editor (and also teacher at the Oporto Faculty of Fine Arts). He has won several awards, both national and international, for his art. He also develops, away from the small art-world, an independent career as an artist, through painting and sculpture, which contributes to one massive body of work, harmoniously influencing one another.

gemeoluisoriginais.com

Manual (P156-157)

Manual is a design and visual communication studio. Their work strives to uncover the intangible essence of a brand and express it through unique visual solutions. Through their process of conceptual design thinking, they help businesses and organizations articulate their unique offerings, giving them more value and distinction.

While they are passionate about design, and continually push themselves and their clients, they like to be collaborative and flexible in their approach. They work with a broad range of clients – from startups, to the world's most revered brands – and maintain a consistently high level of execution and production across print, packaging, and digital media.

Manual practices its craft in San Francisco, California.

manualcreative.com

Manuel Dall'Olio (P216- 217)

Manuel is a graphic designer. In 1994 he started working with communication agencies, companies, artists, and publishers, and he developed a multidisciplinary attitude and approach to design. In 2001, he founded Trelink Intermedia network with designers from the world of communication, design, fashion, and photography.

In 2012, with his wife Mirit Wissotzky, he opened Dina&Solomon, graphic design duet, their studio in Bologna.

He teaches art direction and graphic design in Accademia di Belle Arti di Bologna. He is also a member of AIAP and Icograda.

www.manueldallolio.com/

Matías Fiori (P216- 217)

Matías is a young and fresh graphic designer from Uruguay, with clients all around the world, including Barcelona, England, Brazil, and many countries. He is co-founder of re-robot studio, based in Montevideo, Uruguay.

www.matiasfiori.com / www.re-robot.com

Mayúscula Brands (P134-137)

Mayúscula is a design studio in Barcelona founded by Rocío Martinavarro, specializing in the creation of brands of any complexity and format. Mayúscula in Spanish is an upper case character, a majuscule used to start a sentence or to remark on a concept. It stands out, and that's their main goal for their clients and brands: to exceed the average, using creativity as a strategic tool.

In recent years, their design has helped start-ups like Obbio biologic market, and Kuwaity Zeri Crafts, as well as established companies such as Neinver, the Chinese textile brand Phoenix Village, or the Dutch agency Edenspiekermann. Rocío Martinavarro has over ten years of experience working in New York, Amsterdam, and Barcelona, for companies like Summa Brand Consultancy (National Design Prize), Patrick Thomas, and Edenspiekermann, designing visual identities such as the Spanish Broadcast Corporation (RTVE), la Caixa Savings Bank, Barcelona TV, and Adif o Mútua Terrasa, among others.

www.mayuscula.es

Michael Pharaoh (P130-131)

Michael Pharaoh is a graphic designer based out of Hamilton, New Zealand. He has had a deep, undying passion for all forms of design since he can remember. Whenever he is not actually designing, he is thinking about new projects or clients he'd like to work on. Currently, he is working with international and national clients, and is continuing to expand his client base. He specializes in branding, retouching, and photography.

michaelpharaoh.co.nz

Mind Design (P142-145)

Established in 1999, Mind Design is an accomplished design consultancy that specializes in the development of visual identities, which includes print, web, and interior design. The studio is run by Holger Jacobs and Stewart Walker. Combined, they have more than 20 years experience, and have worked for a wide range of clients, from start-ups to established international companies. Their work has been showcased in various publications and they are regularly invited to give talks. Holger also teaches design at the University of Applied Science in Düsseldorf.

Their approach combines hands-on craftsmanship, conceptual thinking, and most importantly, intuition. They never follow a standard formula and often develop visual ideas on the basis of research into production processes or the use of unusual materials. Depending on the demands of a project, they take advantage of their large network of creative professionals to maximize its potential.

www.minddesign.co.uk

mousegraphics (P128-129)

Design is an endless exercise in communication. mousegraphics is a creative office that realizes this basic principle in a way that concerns each one of its partners/clients separately. This consistent approach has been rewarded with a significant circle of longstanding cooperation, and has also resulted in new and successful professional relationships in a variety of applications within the design field. With a creative team consisting of seven designers, an illustrator, a photographer, a creative strategist, and an office manager, mousegraphics works together with its clients as much in the development of full strategic proposals and plans, as in the realization of targeted, partial applications. mousegraphics has a considerable expertise in packaging design. In fact, a plethora of prestigious international awards and publications have placed the agency among the most interesting, trustworthy, and better technologically equipped to creatively manage food imaging in particular, and in all related levels of communication (logotyping, packaging, development of promotional material et.al.).

mousegraphics is a member of EDEE, the Greek association of advertising and communication agencies, and also member of Design lobby.

www.mousegraphics.gr

Ohmybrand (P058-059)

Ohmybrand studio offers conceptual solutions that have a beautiful design on the outside, and an idea inside – the solutions that execute the tasks of the brand.

www.ohmybrand.ru

OR Shaaltiel (P194-195)

OR Shaaltiel is a graphic design student at WIZO Haifa Academy of Design based in Haifa, Israel.

www.behance.net/or_shaaltiel

P576 (P032-035, 160-161)

P576 is a design studio based in Bogotá, Colombia. They believe that through aesthetics they can help make a more beautiful and honest world.

www.p576.com

Pearlfisher (P174-175)

Pearlfisher is a leading international independent design agency, established in 1992 by designers Jonathan Ford and Karen Welman, and Managing Partner, Mike Branson.

With studios in London and New York, Pearlfisher has a global reputation for creating commercially effective, future-focused design for today's most powerful and loved brands – Challengers & Icons.

www.pearlfisher.com

Pi6 Communication Design (P138-141)

Pi6 is an Athens-based communication design studio, founded in 2005 by Rena Chrysikopoulou and Michael David Ochs. Providing a wide range of design services, pi6 mainly focuses on corporate and editorial design projects.

Pi6's work is characterized by a careful analysis of

the projects' content, which serves as the starting point and basis for each design process. Coming from a multicultural background, Pi6 is equipped with a keen understanding of cultural differences in communication and is aware of the sociocultural responsibility of design. Pi6 works collaboratively with experts in Greece and Germany across various media, thus offering complete services depending on the requirements of each project. Their work has been awarded by the most prestigious design competitions and poster biennales, and has been published in national and international media.

www.pi6.gr

Point-Blank Design Ltd. (P082-083)

Point-Blank Design Ltd. was founded in 1996, providing end-to-end design solutions, from brand identity to interior design for clients from corporate, property, leisure, retail, and restaurants.

At Point-Blank Design, identity program and spatial design is a sophisticated matter of structuring visible and intangible elements, then accentuating the functionality and human experience of a product or service with unsurpassed creativity.

www.pointblank.com.hk

Quinta-feira (P046-047)

Numbers are no longer used to only count and calculate, but they have become appreciated by their own properties. Numbers exist independently of the palpable world, and their study is not affected by the uncertainty of perception. Quinta-feira translates the natural world into numbers, and back again to the natural world, ultimately trying to build worlds out of nature.

www.quinta-feira.org.

Randy Mora (P098-099)

Randy Mora is a freelance illustrator currently living in Bogotá, Colombia.

www.randymora.com

Resatio Adi Putra (P202-203)

Resatio Adi Putra was born in Bandung, Indonesia, and works as a collage artist and graphic designer. He combines collage art and graphic design into something unusual. Words that can describe his artworks are: Structured Chaos. His artworks have been featured in Elle, Nylon, America, Jakarta Post Weekender, and Beautiful/Decay. This self-thought guy is now entirely putting his life into visual art.

www.behance.net/resatio / resatio.tumblr.com

RoAndCo (P054-055)

RoAndCo is a multi-disciplinary design studio devoted to holistic branding that serves a range of fashion, art, and lifestyle clients. Led by award-winning Creative Director Roanne Adams, RoAndCo offers design, image, and branding capabilities across a variety of mediums, from print to moving image. By thoughtfully distilling a client's inspirations, ideas, and motivations, RoAndCo generates fresh, sincere, and compelling brand messages that engage and resonate.

roandcostudio.com

Say What Studio (P148-149)

Say What is a graphic design studio based in Paris, run by Benoit Berger and Nathalie Kapagiannidi, who graduated from the ECV School in Paris.

www.saywhat-studio.com

Sciencewerk (P104-105)

Sciencewerk is just an ordinary design studio located in the infamous city of Surabaya, Indonesia. They have been art directing and creating visual identities since 2010.

www.sciencewerk.net

Somewhere Else (P064-065)

Somewhere Else is an ideas-centered design studio. Largely focused on branding strategies and solutions, the studio is also well-versed in all facets of design from art direction, editorial design, and environmental graphics to way finding systems. Somewhere Else is anywhere other than here and now. It is about the constant shift away from the ordinary; the persistent journey to create work that goes beyond the basic need to communicate. Prior to founding Somewhere Else in 2011, Yong spent 4.5 years as a senior designer at Asylum where he crafted a wide spectrum of projects. During his stint at Asylum, his works went on to receive both local and international awards like the One Show, and The Art Directors Club. His works have also been featured in numerous publications worldwide.

www.somewhere-else.info

Sonia Castillo (P158-159)

Sonia Castillo is a freelance designer focused on graphic design and art direction from Spain, who is currently living in Madrid. Sonia studied in both Spain and Germany – Fine Arts at Madrid and the University HAWK in Hildesheim respectively – and her work across graphic design, typography, advertising, and photography shows marked influences from both scenes in which she was immersed. She has been working in different fields of design from corporate design and web to editorial and illustration. She enjoys exploring and experimenting with typography, geometric forms, and photography. Clear concepts, geometry and minimalism are the essentials of her work.

www.soniacastillo.com

Stockholm Design Lab (P072-073)

Stockholm Design Lab is a multidisciplinary design agency. They create brand identities and solutions that build strong customer relationships. They combine strategic insight and proud craftsmanship of many kinds. They don't differentiate between design, architecture, digital applications and other forms of communication. The perception of a brand is dependent on the slightest components. They experiment, build, think, and rebuild. They are organized, and never compromise with the end result of their work. Quality in every component is what creates the experience of the brands they work with.

They are based in Stockholm, but have always operated globally. Their work has been exhibited in New York, London, Tokyo, Berlin, Köln, Helsinki, and Stockholm.

www.stockholmdesignlab.se

Studio Fludd (P204-205)

Studio Fludd is a multidisciplinary creative collective operating since 2008, and currently based in Venice. The group takes its name from the alchemist Robert Fludd, sharing the aim to transmute base matter through the empiric process. The undertaken projects experiment mixtures: from graphic design to illustration, from printing to installation, and self-produced design. The leitmotif of its research is a very fluid approach towards the visual languages, and a vivid interest for craftsmanship. Studio Fludd is Matteo Baratto (1986), Caterina Gabelli (1984), Sara Maragotto (1986), and Valeria Sanguin (1986).

www.studiofludd.com

Substance (P200-201, 228-229)

Substance is an award-winning independent branding and design agency made up of obsessive perfectionists, vivid storytellers, and a surfboard. The agency was founded in Hong Kong by Maxime Dautresme and Florian Michaux in 2009 as a multi-disciplinary agency specializing on brand identity and srategy, advertising, packaging, web and digital, and interior design. They are curious, adaptable, perfectionists, and above all, human.

www.substance.hk/en

The Birthdays™ (P164-165)

The Birthdays™ is the collaboration of Konstantina Yiannakopoulou and George Strouzas, based in Athens, Greece. Sharing time between real life and design. They believe in design as science, in form through composition, in type as form, in symbols, in communication through concept, through justification, and through clarity. They are devoted to working in print design, and they find it more challenging working for small businesses, though they are open to all kinds of requirements. Effective communication, specificity, and uniqueness always remain the goal.

www.behance.net/TheBirthdays

The Composer (P092-093)

Shawn Chow Hung Yun is an independent graphic designer that practices the belief of creating design that stands out, while at the same time treating it as a work of art. Constantly combining concept and techniques to challenge status quo, tackling problems has always been his core of design. Prior to his graduation, and a short stint at Studio MMCMM, he is now undertaking freelance projects, and at the same time enjoying designing under the radar.

thecomposerdesign.tumblr.com

The Creative Method (P098-099)

The Creative Method was established in 2005 with the sole purpose of creating the best designs off the back of even better ideas. The focus has and always will be on creating brands that have impact, standout, a point of difference, and most importantly, brands that work.

Their aim is to stay small and flexible. They believe that by understanding the principles of great design combined with clear and simple ideas they can and do work in any discipline.

Give them a great story, and they will create a

great brand.

www.thecreativemethod.com

The Folks Studio (P122-123)

The Folks Studio is a design practice based in Singapore and was founded by Yang and Siew in 2012. Derived from the Germanic noun "fulka," "folks" means "people," and serves as a constant reminder to us that "people" are at the core of their thinking, and in what they do.

www.thefolksstudio.com

THiNC (P009-011)

Founded in Mexico in 2009, Thinc ® Mx was born as a conceptual laboratory offering holistic design solutions. They think of themselves as a multidisciplinary workshop that brings together method, design expertise, market knowledge, solid research, and good old fashion creative talent.

From the lines and angles of the blueprint, to the tangible design and communication solutions offered to their clients, they take pride in the creative process that ads value and beauty to every project, product, or brand.

www.thincmx.com

Tommy Li Design Workshop Ltd. (P009-011)

Tommy is the branding designer/consultant, and is renowned for his "Black Humor" and "Audacious Visual" designs. Spanning Hong Kong (China), Mainland China, Japan, and Italy, he is one of the few designers to have penetrated the international market. Having received over 580 awards, he held his 20 years exhibition "Visual Dialogue" in 2010. Tommy Li Design Workshop was selected by "Chinabico.com" as one of the top 10 Branding Companies in China. He obtained the "Gold Pencil" from "The One Show" (NY) in 2007, and was nominated for the "World Outstanding Chinese Award" from the World Chinese Association.

www.tommylidesign.com

Tore Cheung (P020, 021, 022-023, 024-025)

Tore Cheung Siu Ho (aka Tore) was born in Hong Kong in 1984. He graduated from The Hong Kong Polytechnic University majoring in visual communication, and is currently working as a fabric print, and fashion designer.

Apart from his versatile nature, he focuses on art, creating acrylic-based paintings that heavily reference found images from his collection. Treating the process of creating as a treasure hunt, he looks for things that he could borrow and steal. He is particularly interested in seeing how unique delights from different objects are brought together, how beauty and humor emerge accidentally to question the constructed.

Tore believes that by abandoning one's craftsmanship from time to time, one could work more towards the emotional response. The finished pieces are often reflections of his subconscious, other than conscious constructions.

torecheung.com

Total Identity (P196-197)

Total Identity is a creative consultancy. Based on design thinking, we build strong identities. Total Identity was founded in 1963 by Wim Crouwel, Benno Wissing, Friso Kramer, and Paul and Johannes Schwartz, and has developed epic design programs like Schiphol Airport, SHV, Randstad, and Stedelijk Museum Amsterdam. Recently Total Identity established projects for LG Electronics (Korea), CJ, Zumla (Moscow), Vaillant (Germany), Powel (Norway), and Brik (Brussels).

www.totalidentity.nl

Tsto (P068-069)

Tsto is a design agency focusing on visual concepts and art direction. They help their clients define and communicate their identity and message by coming up with ideas, and visualizing them. Their approach is thorough and hands-on. They tackle an assignment by first taking it apart to its bare essentials, and then building it in a new way that best serves the client. This design philosophy lets them go deeper than the surface, to the essence of each case. Through the varied skills of their designers they find the best-suited tools to bring their ideas to life. They do it in a way that focuses on the whole, but with attention to all details. Tsto combines thorough, to-the-point design thinking with a craftsman's can-do attitude. They also work with other proven professionals in whatever media the work requires. Tsto was founded by Johannes Ekholm, Jonatan Eriksson, Inka Järvinen, Matti Kunttu, Jaakko Pietiläinen, and Antti Uotila.

www.tsto .org

Viktor Matic (P044-045)

Viktor Matic is an Italian-based designer, ideas and concept developer, project manager, and cultural entrepreneur. He works in different media on a range of personal and commissioned projects. He finished his bachelor degree in product and communication design in Bozen-bolzano in July 2011. During his studies he spent an exchange year in Jerusalem, and in Istanbul. He is able to communicate in English, German, Italian, and Croatian. He likes things that express an artistic language. He is trying hard to develop his own way of thinking, and his own style in creative production.

www.viktormatic.com

Wallnut (P152-153, 154-155)

Founded in 2007, Wallnut is a graphic design, textile, and branding studio specializing in interdisciplinary projects. Run by Colombian graphic designer, Cristina Londoño, it has a reputation for generating contemporary works developed from a profound passion for color, an obsession for detail, and a lust for research, all applied to concepts, surfaces, fashion, prints, and interiors, among others.

wallnutstudio.com

WeLoveNoise (P028-029)

WeLoveNoise is the creative outlet of Luke Finch. An interactive art director from Manchester, England with a passion for brand, design, and human behavior. His website features the commercial, experimental, and playful works that span a diverse client base throughout an array of different industries.

www.welovenoise.com

Werksemd (P038-039, 040-041, 042-043, 056-057)

Werksemd is a studio for media, independent applications of ideas, and creative direction. By means of systematic intuition, visual discussion, intended distraction, and chaotic precision, they invent, develop, and renew businesses, brands, products, and experiences, commissioned as well as independent work.

www.werksemd.no

Work in Progress (P178-181)

Work in Progress is a multidisciplinary design studio. They create effective and captivating design solutions based on conceptual thinking, great attention to detail, and high levels of craft and finishing. They believe that it is good concepts that dictate form, and these can translate into any media. Their work and style is therefore as varied as their clients, covering all aspects, from brand strategy and positioning, identity, art direction, digital media, through to packaging, signage, and print. It is designed to function across all applications – digital, analogue, and environmental.

The inspiration they gain from their self-initiated projects flows over to their commissioned work.

workinprogress.no

Zafeiriadis Christos (P109)

Zafeiriadis studied Graphic Design (BA) at the Technological Institution of Athens, and is currently working at Bob Studio. He likes collaborating with other designers, illustrators, printers, and artists.

www.behance.net/czaf

Zé Studio (P172-173)

Zé Studio is a Sydney-based studio that creates valuable design experiences, and delivers unique solutions to clients. Remaining true to design that is informed and well-considered – their design leaves no excess.

Zé Studio was initiated by Joe Tarzia in early 2011 and began as an exploration of well communicated design. With a passion for the arts and culture, they strive to grow their involvement in this sector, and continue to work on identities and brands of any scale.

ze-studio.com

ACKNOWLEDGEMENTS

We would like to express our gratitude to all of the designers and companies for their generous contribution of images, ideas, and concepts. We are also very grateful to many other people whose names do not appear in the credits but who made specific contributions and provided support. Without them, the successful completion of this book would not have been possible. Thanks especially to all of the contributors for sharing their innovation and creativity with all of our readers around the world. Our editorial team includes editor Queenie Wu and book designer Ayuu(Oil-Z), to whom we are truly grateful.